Just A Housewife

Rakesh Varma is an IAS officer. He is an alumnus of Lucknow University, having done his B.Sc., M.A. (anthropology), MBA and doctorate in sociology. He has also done his master's in public policy from LKY School of Public Policy, National University of Singapore. He is a government of India-recognized leadership expert and trainer and recipient of the National Award for Excellence in Training. He has been a guest faculty at various training institutes.

Rakesh Verma is an IAS officer [illegible] an alumnus of [illegible] University [illegible], USA [illegible] and [illegible] in [illegible]. He has also done his master's in public policy from [illegible] National University of Singapore. He is a [illegible] leadership expert and [illegible] Award for Excellence in Training. He has been a guest faculty at various training institutes.

Just A Housewife

Rakesh Varma

RUPA

Published by
Rupa Publications India Pvt. Ltd 2019
7/16, Ansari Road, Daryaganj
New Delhi 110002

Sales centres:
Allahabad Bengaluru Chennai
Hyderabad Jaipur Kathmandu
Kolkata Mumbai

ISBN: 978-93-5333-714-8

First impression 2019

10 9 8 7 6 5 4 3 2 1

Printed at HT Media Ltd, Gr. Noida

Disclaimer

First things first, the book that you are holding in your hand is a work of fiction. Names, characters, businesses, places, events, locales and incidents are either the products of the author's imagination or used in a fictitious manner. Any resemblance to actual persons, living or dead, or actual events is purely coincidental. The treatment of all the characters are as per the demand of the story. The author does not intend to outrage, insult, wound or hurt any religion or the religious sentiments, beliefs or feelings of any person(s) or class or community or gender.

Those who understand fiction will never judge and those who judge will never understand. An open mind looks at things in ways that closed ones never can. Happy reading!

Contents

1

A Starry Night

Venue: Grand Hyatt, Mumbai

The twinkling stars spread across the black velvet of the night sky reflected the shimmering stars below. The political bigwigs, the powermongers from the business circuit, the who's who from the dazzling world of Bollywood, the influential bureaucrats and the corporate honchos, all had descended at the Grand Hyatt that evening to attend the much-touted event of the twenty-first century—The Women Achievers Awards.

These days, it's 'the in-thing' to support anything that has the name of a woman or a girl attached to it. Else, you are labeled as a woman-hater, as being regressive or masochist. Nevertheless, nothing could take away the sheen and excitement that this evening promised.

The atmosphere was one of elation and whilst the select guests flowed through the massive hall, a young, modulated voice directed the attention of everyone towards the well-lit stage.

'Hello, everyone! My name is Purabi Roy and I am your host for this evening,' she energetically started with her speech, as all eyes were locked on her—their beautiful host. 'It's a phenomenal night as we are about to honour our women achievers. Indeed, it is a woman's world that we live in and I can proudly say that we certainly do not need a man to fulfill our dreams. We women are self-sufficient. In fact, there is no greater pillar of stability than a strong, independent and educated woman, and I, Purabi Roy, feel privileged to be presenting these awards tonight.'

The crowd broke into a thunderous applause. The audience, that by and large comprised female invitees, looked at Purabi in sheer admiration as she continued with her speech.

'Today, we have amongst us a very gorgeous and talented lady of repute. We all know her and have loved her for her spirit and guts. She is elegant. She is stunning. She is a renowned name in the film industry. Please join your hands in welcoming the very beautiful Pallavi Chhabra. I request her to present these prestigious awards to the deserving divas.'

Pallavi Chhabra, who was an actress of international fame, walked in amidst the pool of well-known personalities. Dressed in a red, off-shoulder Manish Malhotra gown, she looked exquisite. Her skin was flawless and shone like a star. In spite of her 'rumoured' age, she still seemed to have the exuberance of youth and radiated beauty in totality. The crowd welcomed her with a thunderous round of applause as the gorgeous heart-stopper took her place on the ornamented stage, with strobes of light flashing all around her.

'Hello, Mumbai!' she addressed throatily with an

infectious smile. 'I am pleased to be a part of this award function tonight. To present these awards is an honour in itself. Today, I have achieved all the worldly pleasures that a man craves for, but there was never a man behind my resounding success. I struggled all alone through the toughest times of my life. There are many men who will not be able to digest such a thing because they think that we women need them at every step of our lives. Whether in the household or business or profession, we can never flourish without the emotional, financial or physical help from a man; that is what a majority of the men think. Friends, we don't often talk about men being imprisoned by gender stereotypes, but I can see that they are. Let me tell you something. I have never felt the need of a man in my life and there never has been one. I can handle my issues alone and I pride myself on being independent and capable. That's the reason why I feel so connected to the ethos behind this award and hence, the pleasure of being invited here is way beyond words.'

While the crowd was enraptured by her beauty, she continued with her eyes shining brightly and voice steady. 'At this age, I know what suits me and what does not. I don't need a man to critique my outfit or hairstyle before I step out of my house. I am grown up enough to ask for directions when I am lost and I don't need a man who stays lost for hours. It may sound weird when I say that I like my bathroom sink to be sparkly and clean, and I do not want any man to leave foamy bristles all over it.' With a smirk, she continued, 'Of course, I can cook a meal without using every pot and pan in the kitchen. I don't need a man to turn it into a bombsite.' The entire hall was filled with laughter.

'So, you see, I don't want a man to mess up my life, and this, I guess every modern woman sitting here agrees with. This is my life and I have the right to live it the way I want to. I have always been surrounded by independent women who have thrived and shone in everything they have done. Being raised by such women, I have come to realize that you don't need a man to tell you that you are beautiful, or even pay your expenses. On an ending note, if you are such a woman of substance, a feminist, I applaud you. Being independent is a beautiful feeling and hats off to such women who have proved themselves without any external support.' As Pallavi concluded her speech, the crowd broke into a deafening applause.

'Thank you, Pallavi. We are really honoured to have you here. You are truly an inspiration to many,' said Purabi as the two exchanged quick smiles. 'Moving forward, we call on stage Mrs Barkha Malhotra and Ms Aradhya Sharma to receive the most coveted award of the evening, The Women Achievers Awards, in the category of private and government sector, respectively. From the many nominations that we have received so far, the jury has decided on these two names and I request Ms Pallavi to present the trophy to them.'

The trophy—a golden statute of a woman holding up a sparkling crystal globe—was handed over to Pallavi.

'Friends, let me take the privilege of introducing you to the winners. Mrs Barkha Malhotra, Vice President of Fashionista Ventures Private Limited, a well-known name in the fashion industry. She has toiled hard in her life to achieve this position and remarkably, is the youngest of all the VPs present here. Her untiring efforts have helped the organization touch the sky and this is the reason why the jury has chosen her for this prestigious award in the private sector.'

The trophy was handed over to Barkha, a gorgeous woman with an attractive figure. Dressed in a black one-piece suit with noodle straps and matching stilettos, she looked every bit a model herself. There was confidence and a look of pride on her face as she held the trophy in her hands.

'The next name that we have in this category is Ms Aradhya Sharma.' As Purabi announced the name of the winner, a woman in her mid-thirties walked towards the stage.

Aradhya's alluring figure of 34-30-36 was clearly visible through the pink chiffon saree, which she accessorized with a string of pearls. The attire accentuated her beautiful curves. Very elegantly, she took to the stage, making furious attempts to hide the uneasiness that had by then triumphed over her pretty face.

'Ms Sharma,' said Purabi, 'has been working for the past ten years with a government organization of repute. She lost her husband twelve years back and has two lovely daughters to look after. In spite of the irreparable loss, she managed to complete her education and at present, is a soft skills trainer. She is helping many to groom their personalities for a better future. This award is for her exemplary contribution to the government sector.'

The shutterbugs couldn't have enough of the two gorgeous winners as they stood on the dais, beaming with pride. As they climbed down the stairs, a swarm of admiring bees surrounded them. Not a stranger to each other, they exchanged a quick glance before turning around to answer the eager mediapersons.

'Barkha, how are you feeling on winning this prestigious award?' a lady journalist, along with her team of photographers fenced Barkha as Aradhya voluntarily excused herself from the crowd.

'It feels great!' she replied with a smile.

Barkha Malhotra was the wife of Aneesh Malhotra, the technical director of M/s SAM Constructions Private Limited, a well-known company in Gurgaon. But her identity was not confined to just that. She was the vice president of Fashionista Ventures Private Limited, a prominent name in the fashion industry. She was not only charming and blessed with a pleasing personality, but was equally successful in her own field. She deserved every bit of the attention and every award that was bestowed on her. She had made her own identity without being indebted to her husband for that. She had also made her presence felt in social media by updating her name from Mrs Barkha Aneesh Malhotra to simply Barkha Malhotra. Well, she deserved that! The way she addressed the masses displayed the level of confidence that she possessed.

'So, Mrs Barkha, how's your husband doing?' the journalist questioned.

'Oh! Presently he is in Italy, for a business project,' Barkha replied with a tone that reflected pride.

'Yes, yes. How can I forget? Both of you are in the newspapers and magazines almost every other day.'

Barkha smiled in response and excused herself to catch up with the other prominent ladies of the town. She was enviously greeted by many and a lady in her late forties, draped all over in white, questioned her as she took a seat next to her. 'Barkha, what about that contract to construct a flyover in the city? We have also placed our bid and your secretary ensured it will be ours.'

It seemed from her words that the colour of her soul was just the opposite of her dress. But that's how people are. Two sides of the same coin. Isn't it?

'Oh yes! I remember, Mrs Chugh,' Barkha replied coldly. 'The secretary has informed me. I have already spoken to one of my contacts who happens to be the right-hand man of the minister in charge. He has been well paid in advance. Don't worry! Your job will be done. And mind you, I don't step back from my words. Once a deal, always a deal! So, you need not remind me every time we meet.'

It was that self-pride in her that made sure not to let anyone raise their pitch against her.

'That's why we trust you, dear. We know our money is in safe hands,' the woman replied, taken aback by the cold response.

'Thank you for trusting. An acceptance letter will be issued to you soon,' Barkha said as she got up to take a seat somewhere in the front row.

'Huh! What did I say wrong? She was so cold to me,' muttered the frustrated woman behind Barkha's back.

∾

It was not long after that when Barkha and Aradhya came face to face with each other. They had successfully managed to excuse themselves from their respective groups of supporters and were soon found hugging each other.

'Where have you been all these years, Aradhya? I have been looking for you everywhere and I am so glad that we met, finally!' Barkha said loosening her grip on Aradhya. 'I am stunned to know about your husband, dear. Just don't know what to say. The last time I saw you, it was as a radiant bride, all adorned with red sindoor.' Barkha was inquisitive to know more and more about her long-lost friend and the absence of sindoor on her face troubled her.

'Don't feel sad for me, Barkha. I have fond memories of him. I also have my two daughters...'

'But look at you, my gorgeous girl!'

Their conversation was abruptly cut off by an ever-hungry photographer. 'Mrs Barkha, can we have you here for a cover photograph?'

It's hard to keep away from people when you are at an important position in the society. Yes! Riches do affect your personal interactions and so was the case with Barkha. She wanted to catch up more with her friend but succumbed to the request of the journalist.

'Yes. Coming!' She rushed back for the photo op, handing over her visiting card to Aradhya. 'Promise me that you will call me once the party gets over.'

'Promise!' Aradhya replied with a smile and watched Barkha leave in haste, carrying with her a piece of paper with Aradhya's number scribbled on it.

2

School for Neighbours

Every year, the beginning of December brings with it pangs of anxiety and a whirlwind of emotions for the parents of children aged between three and four. The chilly winter months are not known as much for their showers as they arc for the pre-admission blues that these parents face. Every city in India that has a substantial number of convent schools faces the turbulence as and when December knocks on their door. There is a mad rush for admission forms. Most of the times there is practically no announcement beforehand regarding the form dates, only a question mark that gives a remarkable boost to the stress levels in such parents who wonder and wait for the forms to arrive.

The struggle doesn't end there. After you get hold of the form by waiting in long queues, and not to mention the disruption of one's normal work routine almost every other day, you need to submit the form to the authorities, and they need to be absolutely flawless! A single mistake, however minor it may be, may result in an outright rejection of the form. If the entire admission process is defined in a word, it would be—'irksome'. That is true for not only the parents but also for their children, who are made to join pre-nursery classes, tuitions and what not to focus on the syllabus for their admission tests. Not only this, the parents at times even resort to medication and counselling activities that would help them withstand the pre-admission blues of their little ones. So, this is how it goes for parents in India. December and pre-admission struggles go hand in hand, resulting in a most complex situation—that of BATTLE ADMISSION!

The residence of Aneesh and Barkha Malhotra was not untouched by this admission disaster. Bungalow No. 401. The lights were on since early morning. It was yet another important day for Mrs Barkha Malhotra. Barkha was sitting in the corner teaching Nivedita, their three-old-daughter, early in the morning.

'Why does she have to wake up so early, Barkha? She is too small and it's so cold outside.' Aneesh complained to his wife as he clutched his quilt with both hands and waited for Barkha to relent.

'It's admission time in a few days, Aneesh. Don't you know that?' Barkha shot back, rather scornfully.

Of late, this was normal behavior for Barkha and Aneesh was by now used to seeing his wife like this.

'I also have to leave for work but before that, I have to ensure that Nivedita revises her homework,' Barkha continued. She was a very passionate worker and her work always had an upper hand, including on her family.

'Why don't you take a break from your career? Nivedita is still very young. Don't you think you need to spend more time with your child rather than the maid you have for her?' Aneesh asked, agitated.

'The maid takes good care of Nivedita and besides, I don't want to sit back at home, like the bahenji. I have a reputation and I have to maintain that.'

Barkha had her own choices and ways in life. Aneesh knew she could sacrifice everything, but not her job. He didn't want her to leave her career, but yes, he wanted her to dedicate more hours to their little daughter, who was growing up to the whims and fancies of the hired help. Aneesh chose instead to stay quiet. He knew his suggestions were always rejected by his dear wife.

'Anyways, since the very beginning, I have always wanted the best for her. And that has to start with the best school here, Aneesh.' Saying this, Barkha stormed out of the room, leaving behind a speechless husband who stared after her and succumbed to her harsh words, as always.

൭

The days that followed that conversation were not good either; neither for little Nivedita, nor for Barkha, nor for Aneesh. With each passing day, the anxiety and eagerness dwelling in Barkha's heart grew. This eventually lead to the increase in workload for Nivedita, whose play hours were soon cut short and replaced by all sorts of 'curriculum'. The constant pressure and nagging by Barkha to get Nivedita admitted to the best school in town led to frequent fights between the couple. It seemed all the topics other than Nivedita's admission, had come to an end. Aneesh had very obediently abided by his wife's wishes when it came to shortlisting of the schools for their daughter. He knew Barkha, being a mother, would always choose the best for her. Days flew by and it was soon time for Nivedita to sit for her admission exams. She did equally well in all her tests, for all the schools. In fact, to put it correctly, she *had to* come out with flying colours, thanks to the constant pressure her mother had put on her.

Not only tuitions and studies at home, but to Aneesh's bewilderment, the little girl was also coaxed into registering for pre-nursery coaching in the morning and evening hours which were conducted by Ms Ramanna Raza, a teacher in one of the prestigious schools in town. There was barely an inch of space left in the teacher's overly crowded room where preschoolers were taught all that was meant for a first grader. Aneesh hated this system since the very beginning and had always wanted the little one to learn things on her own, rather than from the tuition classes. This constant pressure to perform, according to him, was too much for a three-year-old, and rightly so. What bothered Aneesh even more now was Barkha's desire to choose the best (high-end) amongst the already chosen schools. He knew his wife wouldn't be satisfied with just the good one! It had to be the best—always.

∾

'Are you even listening to me, Aneesh?' Barkha asked in a tone that sounded offended rather than stern as the duo was having their morning cup of tea.

Aneesh kept his newspaper aside and looked at Barkha, who was all set to blow him up with her fiery words.

'Yes, I am listening. I told you that I cannot help with

the admission once the entrances and the interviews are over.'

'But, Aneesh…'

'I have to leave for office now. I am getting late.' Aneesh stood up in haste, not letting Barkha trigger any other argument that he might not be able to defend.

Aneesh was clearly irritated. The day of the interview and the conversation thereafter were still fresh in his mind. It was a Tuesday morning. He and Barkha were headed for an interview following a call from the principal's office of St Atnes. Nivedita had cleared the entrance test to the school and that was the next step in her admission process.

'Welcome, Mr and Mrs Malhotra,' Sister Mariam, the principal, greeted them as they took their seats in her office. 'I congratulate you on your child's success in our entrance exams. She did extremely well. Sister Mariam's smile and her calm face made Aneesh relax a bit and eased him during this traumatic phase.

'Thank you, Ma'am,' he replied, exchanging smiles with Sister Mariam, who ordered the peon to fetch two glasses of water for the guests.

'So, tell me something about you both,' Sister Mariam asked.

'Well, I am a technical man, Ma'am—' Aneesh started to answer but was interrupted by Barkha.

'And I am the vice president of Fashionista Ventures.'

'Oh! Fashionista! That's a well-known name,' sister Mariam smiled at Barkha, impressed.

'Yes, and I take care of Nivedita at home too,' Barkha continued.

'That's really appreciable. Being a working woman, you

have been able to take good care of your child.'

'Thank you and I want the best things for my daughter too.'

Sister Mariam smiled back at her remark and turned to Aneesh. 'So, Mr Malhotra, what do you do?'

'I am the technical director in a reputed construction company…'

'You must have heard of SAM Constructions,' Barkha interrupted again.

She never failed to flaunt their accomplishments. Aneesh, on the other hand, felt disgusted. SAM Constructions was a well-known name in the construction industry and their buildings feats included some of the most exquisite infrastructures in the town. He didn't want anyone to be partial to the family because of their societal status.

'Oh yes! I know. That's a renowned name. So, Mr Aneesh, you work with that company?'

Aneesh nodded in affirmation.

The questions that followed after the basic introduction were basically related to their family background, responsibility towards the child, opinion about the school and more. The calm and composed nature of the principal put them at ease. There were no direct and personal questions, only the relevant ones to understand the parents' outlook towards their child and the school.

'Thank you, Mr and Mrs Malhotra. It was nice to meet you. We have few more interviews lined up now. We'll inform you accordingly about your child's selection,' Sister Mariam said as she accompanied the couple to the school gate.

'It was nice of her to treat us like that. What do you think,

Barkha?' Aneesh asked once they were seated in their car.

'Hmm...but I have heard that La Martiniere is the best school here. I hope Nivedita gets admission there. My friend's children are in that school and the management is equally good,' Barkha muttered, flipping through the pages of a fashion magazine.

There was silence in the car on their way home. Aneesh knew there was nothing he could do to put some sense into Barkha, so he chose to remain quiet.

ᔕ

The day after the interview with Sister Mariam, both Aneesh and Barkha got ready. Barkha had instructed him about the clothes that he had to wear, the shoes that he ought to put on and even the watch that he was to wear. They were, in fact, headed to Barkha's most preferred destination in terms of the schools of the town, which was a few metres away. Barkha even instructed Aneesh about the things that he needed to say and how to behave before the principal.

Barkha gave him a quick look as they got down from their car. Aneesh felt like a sacrificial lamb taken to be slaughtered. The principal of La Martiniere was Ma'am Hiller. They had to wait for an hour outside her office before being called upon for the interview session. Aneesh overheard a woman who had come out of the principal's office blurting to her better half, 'What exactly did she want to prove when she questioned me for being a housewife? Have I committed a crime?'

Aneesh and Barkha entered the principal's office after a while. A lady in her mid-forties wearing thick gold-rimmed glasses signaled them to take a seat. Aneesh and Barkha took their seats as Ma'am Hiller scribbled something on a piece of paper.

'So, your child has been selected in our entrance exams. How do you feel?' she asked without even looking at them.

Aneesh felt the slight; the arrogance of the principal was palpable.

'Oh! It's a great school and I feel really happy for my child,' Barkha was quick to reply on their behalf.

'Good! So, what do you people do?' asked Ma'am Hiller, raising her brows and adjusting her specs.

'I am the vice president of Fashionista Ventures and my husband is the director of SAM Constructions Private Limited. I hope you have heard the names,' Barkha replied, smilingly.

'Yes. I have. But why doesn't your husband answer my questions?' Ma'am Hiller questioned.

Barkha nudged Aneesh slyly that made him alert.

'It's nothing like that, Ma'am…' Aneesh said.

'Leave it, Mr Malhotra. I don't want an explanation. Tell me something about your child and how do you manage her at home?'

And so the next question followed, and the next, and the next. The interview session went on for almost half an hour.

'Thank you, Mr and Mrs Malhotra. You may leave now. You'll be informed if we select your child.' Ma'am Hiller signaled the couple to leave as she got busy scribbling on that piece of paper again.

'She was stern!' Aneesh remarked as they both stepped out of the principal's room.

'Yes. But she's the principal of the best school. Anyways,

I want Nivedita to be admitted to this one.'

Memories from his past hovered over Aneesh. His ideologies made him a strong opponent of the Do-or-Die admission situations. He strongly felt the need of schooling but not at the cost of one's own life or that of your child's. He remembered Barkha's words at every stage of Nivedita's admission process and wondered how the expectations of parents had changed gradually over a period of time.

'Sa'ab ji... Your office has come,' addressed his driver from the front seat, jolting him out of his reverie.

'Hmm...' Aneesh replied in a dull voice. 'Pick me up at 9 tonight.'

Time passed but the problems and complications of life remained the same. In fact, with each passing day, it only grew worse. Like any other day, today too, Aneesh was seeing red over a squabble with his dear wife, Barkha. As always, a conversation had triggered an argument between the couple relating to the admission of their daughter in a prestigious school, which according to Barkha was 'the best'. Like any other day, she fought with Aneesh with their little daughter standing near her as a mute spectator, unable to comprehend why her parents were always angry with each other.

'I want the best school in the city for my daughter. Mrs Dixit and my friends told me that La Martiniere is the best, so it has to be La Martiniere and nothing else,' Barkha shouted, clenching her fist in anger.

'Even I want that, Barkha. We have filled the forms for the best schools in Lucknow. I just want you to cooperate with me and not make a fuss about this anymore,' Aneesh replied, knotting his tie.

'Am I making a fuss? Really, Aneesh? I just want you to talk to the trustee or whoever and get it done by hook or crook. I ain't disagreeing that the other schools are good too, but this one is the best. And I want the best for my daughter. Do you get that? Nothing but the best.'

Barkha was adamant to get her daughter admitted to the best school. She was not the kind of person to ever settle for less. Being first and the best was the only thing that mattered to her.

'Barkha, don't be so stubborn. Heaven will not fall if Nivedita is not admitted to La Marts. We are trying for all the best schools. Then why to stick to just one? Just because someone told you that it's the best? Nivedita has given her exams and we have given our interviews. Now whatever happens will be the best for our daughter. We as parents need to ensure that Nivedita grows up to be a good human being. Schools, colleges, all are secondary.' Aneesh very sensibly laid down his point before his furious wife, who was by now like a raging bull charging at Aneesh, the matador waving the red flag.

'Knowing that it's the best, I want it anyhow. We have given the interviews for all the schools, as you said…'

'All the schools? No, only the top schools,' Aneesh interrupted.' And I didn't shortlist the schools, you did that yourself.'

'Yes, I did. But is there anything wrong if I insist on one now?' Barkha kept stressing her point, flaring up every now and then. 'All I am saying is use your contacts to ensure our child's selection. Give them money. In fact, give them loads of it, if that's what it takes.'

'Barkha. Don't behave so immaturely. In the first place, you decided the schools. I abided by your decision and stood in the extremely long queues early in the morning, took leaves from my office, in spite of being warned continually. I struggled to get the forms and now when the interviews are over, at least wait for the results. They don't entertain anyone after the interviews.' Aneesh felt miserable. 'Moreover, why start Nivedita's schooling with recommendations and favours? Believe me, God has the best in store for her.'

However much did Aneesh try, there was no way he could make his wife understand the simple logic and philosophies of life.

Barkha was still adamant. 'Aneesh, you are not getting my point. If we sit twiddling our thumbs, waiting for the results, nothing is going to happen. It's the right time to act. What if Nivedita doesn't get selected to La Marts? Then who will be responsible? You cannot just sit back and wait for the results to arrive. You have contacts. Use them. Talk to the principal. Shower them with money. Do anything. Whatever needs to be done, do it. I want my daughter's name in that list.' Barkha stomped her feet and walked out of the room.

This was not the first instance. In all their years of marriage, Aneesh had failed miserably to make his wife understand that life can indeed be simple. She simply wouldn't listen to anything sensible that Aneesh had to say. Being the best or getting the best was all that she could think of. Because of this attitude of Barkha, the couple had always missed out on the small portions of happiness that had come knocking at their door. Only this time, it was about Nivedita's admission.

The fights continued for the rest of the week. Aneesh tried to convince his wife that things were beyond his control but Barkha refused to listen to his pleas and statements.

෴

The D-Day finally arrived. Aneesh silently prayed for his daughter's name to be in the list displayed outside the massive premises of La Martiniere. With Nivedita's roll number scribbled on a small piece of paper, he made his way towards the display board. He too joined the queue of overenthusiastic and nervous parents. He knew that all hell would break loose if the roll number was not there in that list. He knew his whole family would suffer eventually. With these thoughts running through his head, Aneesh began to nervously scroll through the roll numbers. 4,6,7,8,9,10... but roll number 1 was nowhere to be seen. He rechecked the roll number and the display board thrice to ensure that he did not miss it.

'Excuse me...' a lady standing behind him gave him a stern look. 'Are you done? If you don't mind, we also have to check the board.'

'I am s...sorry.'

With a heavy heart, Aneesh stepped back and gave way to the parent.

Nivedita's name was not there in the list and this was enough for his married life to go further downhill. He clenched his fist, holding the paper tightly in his hand and walked out of the school premises. With halts at the other two schools to check their list of selected students, he instructed the driver to drive home. In his heart he knew what was destined to follow.

As expected, he spotted Barkha at the gate as the car made its way to the long driveway.

'What happened? The name is there in the list, na?' Her words tumbled out, giving him no time to ease the blow.

'No.' Aneesh replied as a matter of fact, avoiding any eye contact with Barkha.

'What do you mean by "No"?' she was quick to ask him.

'Nivedita got selected in St Atnes.'

'St Atnes? But I told you to try for La Marts. Didn't I?'

'Barkha, listen to me. St Atnes is an equally good school. You met the principal, right? They'll take good care of our child.'

'Yes, I know. But it's not La Marts.'

'What's there in the name? You had decided the schools. And we are lucky that our daughter has been selected in one of the best schools here.'

'If you had tried, she would have been selected in the leading school, Aneesh. It's all your fault. I told you. But you never listen to me. How will I feel now when someone asks me why I didn't try for the best?'

'Stop it, Barkha. Your "best" tag doesn't work everywhere.' Aneesh was starting to lose his temper. 'Accept the fact that your child will be going to one of the best schools in town. Yes, it is not La Marts, but I don't care and you shouldn't too. St Atnes is the school, and that's what you will tell your friends and well-wishers.'

'If only you had talked to the principal once.'

'Nothing would have happened. These are reputed schools and the mechanism doesn't work as per your fancies. They have strict norms. Moreover, Nivedita got selected to St Atnes based on her merit. It is not easy to get admission there. You know it. We are fortunate enough. Can't you see that?'

'All I know is, Aneesh, you never understand what I say. I believe in the best because I know I am capable of getting it. But you don't seem to get my point because you never try to. You are a backbencher, dear husband, and you make me realize that every time.' Fuming, Barkha left, leaving behind a disheartened husband.

The days that followed after that were as usual horrible for Aneesh. Barkha refused to talk to him. She even made sure that Nivedita didn't interact much with her father. All that was left in the massive building was a discomforting silence. As for Barkha, she soon got busy with her own professional and social life. But she never missed an opportunity to remind her husband about the comments that her so-called well-wishers had made when they found out about Nivedita not being able to secure admission to La Martiniere. All the while, Aneesh would quietly listen to his wife and wait for her to get over this complaining phase. He would constantly try to bring her back to the reality and put some sense and happiness to their ruined and troubled marriage but all went in vain. Never once did Barkha try to get down off her high horse. Barkha Aneesh Malhotra always wanted 'the best', come what may.

3

The Maid Family

(Fifteen years later)

Years passed for Aneesh like a flash. As business grew, he had to locate to Gurgaon. Life in a place like Gurgaon was never fascinating for Aneesh. The multistory buildings, abundant malls, multiplexes, high streets and expensive lifestyle never really thrilled him. What he craved for was inner peace and happiness that were far away from him.

That day was like no other day. Looking out of the window, he wondered how Barkha could be such an exhibitionist. She always wandered in the swamp of glitz and glamour. Two opposite sides of a coin they were. Nothing could fix his perturbed marital life, but Aneesh still seemed determined to do it.

'Here is your drink.' Barkha's rather throaty voice brought him back to the reality.

His wife seemed to enjoy herself a hell lot in that party with free-flowing booze and seemed more than reluctant to go back home.

'No. I am not interested,' Aneesh replied, rather gloomily. 'And I think you need to come home with me now. It's already very late, Barkha.'

'Oh! You are so uninteresting, Aneesh. Try and connect with people here. It's called networking, darling. Life in a corporate sector is all about networking. Don't be a spoilsport.'

'The children are alone at home. I really think we need to leave now. It's already 11.' Aneesh tried to divert Barkha's rather rigid mind from her friends to her family.

His children were at home and his concentration was on them, who were left forlorn by his wife for this nonsense party.

'C'mon. It's only 11. And this party is so much fun. You are sitting so isolated. Look at everyone. They are having so much fun. Get a life, dear hubby,' Barkha replied, almost rebuking Aneesh and all the while typing furiously into her phone. She did not even bother to look at her husband.

'I think the children will be more than happy to see us. We need to give them time too,' he murmured.

The crowd and the chaos in that room bothered him, and he got up to leave.

'Nivedita must be studying for her IIT exams. Leave her alone, Aneesh,' Barkha murmured, trying to fasten her seatbelt.

'I think you need to be with her. And this IIT stuff is beyond my thinking power. I think you need to give her freedom to decide for herself.'

As they made their way home, there was complete silence in the car. There was no point arguing. The thoughts and circumstances were different, but the victim was still the same—Aneesh Malhotra. The days of Nivedita's school admission flashed before his eyes. 'Why do parents plan for their children just to show off to relatives and friends?' Aneesh wondered.

൭

The morning rays of the sun are believed to bring in new hopes and aspirations, but in the household of Aneesh and Barkha Malhotra—ironically named 'Khushi'—it only meant new problems and confrontations. Seeing red over a trivial matter with the housemaid, Barkha dashed out for office, slamming the door behind her. Before leaving, she strictly instructed Nivedita to continue with her preparations for the IIT entrance. What failed to enter Aneesh's *not-so-materialistic mind* was the pressure that Barkha was putting on her 16-year-old to crack this exam. It seemed that IIT was the only option left with their daughter if she had to survive on this planet. He remembered what Barkha had said days back.

'It's not only good for Nivedita, but it is also a matter of prestige for us. Can't you see, Aneesh? After that La Martiniere episode, I cannot face my kitty ladies. Now I won't let it happen again. The sooner you understand this, the better for you.' Saying this, she had left, leaving behind a husband who had waited all his life for a chance to speak.

Children, their admissions and their career choices were all a matter of prestige for his dear wife. She brought everything down to their societal status and their chances of conquering the world. Aneesh had merely become a puppet to her whims and fancies. Aneesh choked with emotion.

'Papa, we want a bigger car to drop us to school and coaching. The old one seems so outdated now. We feel embarrassed in front of our friends. My friend comes in an Audi, and look at poor me, I am stuck with an i10.' Nivedita's sudden demand brought him back to the present.

'Why do you want a new car? Dear, the make of the car you use has no bearing on your preparations. Why do you keep comparing yourself with these rich people? There must also be children coming in cycles and scooters.' Feeling suffocated from within, Aneesh flung his bed sheet to one side and left the room.

He didn't know why he behaved the way he did with his daughter and nor did she. The kids were surely not to be blamed for the strangling environment in their home. Aneesh felt miserable. He felt like he had never before. He remembered how once he had thrashed the little girl at the very tender age of 8 for a mere jar of Nutella that she had finished in two days. Those days were a struggle for him. He was going through a tremendous financial crisis due to the significant downfall in the company returns and he merely could manage two–three Nutellas a day. But Barkha continued with her extravagant expenditures even during those days.

He had been helpless, but now he felt desolated. What had started as a difference of opinion escalated to strong feelings and raised voices. Aneesh could feel something churn in his stomach. He knew things were not on the right track. The once-cheerful Aneesh had become an irritated and a frustrated being in all these years. Every time he tried to discuss and resolve a conflict, there was emotional withdrawal. Whatever the couple was facing was gradually taking a toll on their parenting. The Nutella episode was one such disaster. It all seemed like yesterday.

Barkha's attitude of trying to conquer the world had gradually started to conquer Nivedita's thought process too and there was simply nothing Aneesh could do about it.

The tremendous pressure Nivedita was under made her weak and her father choke with sadness. But Barkha was unaware of all this. All she could see was a bright and non-compromising future for her daughter, who was presently compromising on all her little happiness. For Barkha, IIT had become an obsession and she was tempted ceaselessly to spend a ridiculous amount on Nivedita's tuition and coaching classes. Debarred from all the pleasures and activities of her teenage years, Nivedita stood isolated against her wishes with her entrance books and the constant pressure that her mother put on her. All this was unacceptable to Aneesh. He had a number of times tried to make his wife understand.

'Happiness is much more than cracking an IIT entrance, Barkha. Why do you separate her from her friends? And why put so much pressure on her? Let her live her life the way she wants to,' he would say.

'What do you mean by that? Sky is the only limit for her and IIT is the only way out. Have you seen Mrs Dutta's daughter? She is also doing the same and Mrs Dutta is so very proud of it. She keeps on boasting all the time. And Mrs Mehta…her son has cracked JEE. I also have some prestige in society,' she would answer.

'But why connect your prestige with Nivedita's future?

She is good at Arts and she is a lot interested in it. Why not help her out with a career choice of her own? Why force your opinion on her? You don't have to be an engineer always to be successful.'

'Nivedita is very young and she doesn't know anything.'

'People are not born to just pursue engineering and I would suggest don't follow the herd, instead carve your own niche.'

'I am not interested in your lectures, Aneesh. They do not make sense to me. All I know is that I can decide better for her.'

The arguments never had any conclusions or a full stop. Only the frustration level would seep deep down to Aneesh's heart making him feel more dejected and unwanted in his own home.

If there's one thing worse than a miserable, lonely single person, it's a miserable, lonely married person. People believe that marriage is the cure for loneliness, but the truth is that in this world of pomp and show, isolation has reached the most intimate of human relationships. The truth is that there is nothing more potent than isolation in destroying marriages. Aneesh was stuck in one such. However hard he tried, there was nothing he could do to make his wife happy. She always seemed irked and would fly into fits of rage over seemingly trivial matters. The bathroom episode was one such that Aneesh could recall vividly. Barkha had once locked him in just because he didn't open the washroom window in anticipation of her coming in later. There were many like this. His thoughts and suggestions had no place in his own house.

The same day, seated on a couch with a cup of hot coffee, Aneesh tried to recall his first encounter with Barkha. She was bold and beautiful, and he had instantly fallen in love with her when he saw her for the first time at a five-star hotel. She was the assistant manager there and Aneesh was the regional head of a big MNC. He remembered that day very well. The whole series of events flashed before his eyes. His office had scheduled a corporate meeting at the hotel and he was infuriated by the arrangements there. The cameras, the audio-video system, the lunch, nothing was perfect and since he was in charge of this meet, he got an earful from his seniors.

'We are extremely sorry for the inconvenience, sir. Please calm down. We are checking the wires of the cameras and the audio-video system. It will take some time but not much, we promise,' pleaded the hotel manager, Mr Agnihotri.

'Mr Agnihotri, this was the least that was expected of you. Is this what you call the hospitality of a five-star hotel? Nothing is good over here. Even the lunch was pathetic. I didn't pay less to you people, I guess. The service that we received was intolerable. You knew we had an important meeting today with international delegates. Now how do I explain all this chaos to my seniors? Their meeting has been ruined because of me, or should I say because of YOU.'

'We are very sorry, sir...' Mr Agnihotri apologized, feeling guilty about the whole incident.

'What do I do with your "very sorry, sir" now? Do you realize I could have been sacked because of your disastrous service? Even the food that you served today was stale and had a foul smell,' Aneesh replied in a rage, jerking away all the requests of the hotel manager. 'You just wait and watch, Mr Agnihotri. I am going to withdraw the corporate agreement with your hotel very soon.'

'Please, sir. Give us another chance. We'll rectify it,' requested the baffled manager.

'Give you another chance so that you can screw this further? No, Mr Agnihotri. This agreement needs to come to an end. I am sorry, but I have to do this.'

The troubled manager left immediately to fix things while Aneesh paced around, feeling fires of fury smoldering deep down in his system. As he was about to leave, a silvery voice from behind caught his attention. 'Excuse me, sir!'

He turned around to find a young and beautiful face greeting him with a smile that could easily kill millions.

'Yes?'

'My name is Barkha and I am the assistant manager of this hotel.'

'Please tell me,' Aneesh said, rolling up his sleeves.

'We are very sorry for the inconvenience caused to you. But believe me, we are equally perturbed. We are looking into the matter and hopefully it will be sorted out soon,' Barkha replied softly.

'When, miss? Our meeting is ruined and so is my image. Your hotel management has already screwed it all up,' replied Aneesh morosely.

'I understand, sir, but please give us another chance to put back things to normal for you,' said Barkha rolling her eyes.

It was the first time that Aneesh noticed her prominent features. She was fair, attractive and a good-looking young girl with a height of about 5 ft 5 inches and voluminous long hair. Her structure, probably her curvy body was enough to make heads turn. Aneesh melted. To him, she was like a gush of fresh air that soothed down his aching heart and mind.

Had it not been for this girl, Aneesh would have refused to talk to any of the hotel authorities on this issue.

'I don't know, dear, if I can really help you with this,' he replied softly, bowled over by her ravishing good looks and smart attire of a semi-transparent shirt, which revealed the black bra that she wore underneath, and a black skin-tight skirt that accentuated her curves to the fullest. Aneesh couldn't help but stare at her slightly saggy heavy breasts as she deliberately bent forward to flaunt her assets. As their eyes met, she caught Aneesh having a sneak peek through the topmost button of her shirt that was left undone to display the satin-like skin beneath. She smiled seductively and held his hands in hers. Gently caressing them, she replied, 'Please, sir. For the sake of my job, you need to give us some more time.'

Aneesh felt a tickling sensation, aroused by her soft touch. Planting a soft kiss on his lips, she said, 'I know you'll not put me in a disastrous situation.'

Aneesh's anger vanished into thin air as she held his hands and said, 'Why don't we sit and talk in a room? Please, sir. Everybody is here.'

'I'll not withdraw the agreement, if you insist,' he managed to mutter.

Barkha thanked him coyly and pecked him once again on his cheeks. 'I'll see you after my shift,' saying this, she left, leaving behind Aneesh who was craving for more.

He had instantly developed a liking for her. Everything was crystal clear. From the very first day, he had planned to have her in his arms forever.

൭൭

Despite the fact that Barkha was a simple graduate, and despite the rumors floating around that she had deceived her ex and used the manager to get to this level, Aneesh didn't budge in his idea of marrying her. 'She is the one.' He knew it. So there was no stopping him.

'Barkha, I don't want a working woman to be my wife. I want someone to take care of my family, me and our future children. Once they grow up, you can resume your job. But, I am sorry you'll have to leave your job as of now.' Aneesh had once told Barkha and she had readily succumbed. This was the first and the last time that he remembered her agreeing to his words.

Just a few days after the wedding, Aneesh came to know that she had a friend-cum-ex called Rahul, whom she had left because of his not-so-rich status. He was a conservative kind of guy and in a respectable government service. But his societal status was way behind that of Aneesh and way below Barkha's expectations. All this, he came to know from a very close friend. However, Barkha had denied the fact every time.

'It's just bullshit. You know how much I love you. Don't you?' Her statements always melted his heart and he never ever cared to look at the shadows behind the curtains.

Two years post their marriage was the only period that Aneesh remembered being good in their entire relationship.

Barkha had been quite good for the time being. She remained at home and took good care of the entire family but after the birth of their daughter her simplicity gave way to a troublesome one.

'I get bored here, Aneesh. I have nothing to do after you leave. I want to resume my work and be independent.'

'Nivedita is so young, Barkha. You should be around her. She needs you,' he would protest.

'She can stay with the house maid, but I'll go insane if I stay back like this anymore. This is not my cup of tea. If you'll not allow me, someday or the other I'll commit suicide and you'll be solely responsible for it.'

The constant nagging, threats and persuasion made Aneesh give in to her wishes. After all, he was deeply and madly in love with her. The family was happy and Barkha made it complete. So there was no reason to say no to her. Despite his initial unwillingness, he agreed to her working. Unfortunately or fortunately, that opened the gates of freedom for her. Gradually but steadily, she began climbing new heights. Aneesh was happy for her, but her constantly ignoring him and the family deeply perturbed him.

'Barkha, don't you think you are ignoring us because of your work?'

'No,' the subtle and straightforward reply made him step back.

Barkha's success continued along with the family sufferings. She even faced a miscarriage because of all the ups and downs in her life. The family who was overjoyed at the news of her pregnancy, soon mourned over the loss of the child, but to Barkha, it all seemed normal.

'Things like this happen, Aneesh. Don't be so panicky over a trivial loss. I am sure we have something brighter ahead.'

The birth of their son, Ayaan, brought new responsibilities for Barkha. But happiness was always short-lived for Aneesh. Even the happy atmosphere at home could not bring back the long-lost freshness of his married life. Arguments continued and quarrels became a part of daily routine. Trivial matters were taken outside the building and blown out of proportion. Frequent comparisons were made with people around them.

'Look at Rajesh. He is so practical in life. And look at you!'

'Mrs Gupta was telling me that her husband always takes her out for a holiday once in a month. We don't go anywhere.'

'The lady next door has a very good family. She is indeed very lucky. I wish I were that lucky.'

There was extreme anger and resentment, constant comparisons, and whatever one could think of in their tormented married life. Aneesh was forced to believe that he was 100 percent responsible for whatever was happening. He was also made to feel like a bad person—the only one who was responsible for all their marital problems. And the worst part was that all this happened right in front of their kids, who were the only two lovely reasons for Aneesh to survive in this 'so-called home'.

All this continued without halt and in all this chaos, Aneesh was lost somewhere and his career deteriorated. She would often threaten him with the pretext of domestic violence when he refused to give in to her tantrums. 'Look what you did!' she would yell in the highest pitch possible, deliberately making marks and scars on her body.

Even during the time of financial losses, she refused to cooperate and swiped her credit card without a care. When Aneesh asked her to stop spending frivolously, she labelled him as a 'controlling ass'. Not just that, she even bribed him with sex to get what she wanted and withheld it if she didn't get what she wanted. Anger and irritation in the relationship eventually killed love and sexual feelings.

'No, I am not doing it.'

'No, I am not agreeing to it.'

'No, I am not cumming.'

It seemed that 'no' was the only answer to all that Aneesh had to offer. Barkha was always reluctant to change or even agree in any situation. Her unpredictable moods, temper and inability to control her emotions, among many other things were beyond Aneesh. Years of pent-up frustration, anger and resentment finally led to health problems for Aneesh.

He was driven away from his mental peace. The result being a ruined married life with high frustration levels and a phase of no solution.

All these memories flashed in front of Aneesh's eyes, who held his cup, which was left untouched so far.

'*Sa'ab, coffee thandi ho gai. Garam kar du?* (Sa'ab, your coffee has gone cold. Should I reheat it?),' the maid offered.

'*Nahi* (No).' He kept the cup on the table and left.

4

BYOB: Who Will Bring BONDING?

'Congratulations, Aneesh! You did a fabulous job,' a colleague of Aneesh congratulated him on being declared as the best director amongst the many verticals of their company.

It was the eve of their annual meet and one by one everyone applauded Aneesh for his achievement. It was indeed a big one. He had really worked day in and out. While everyone looked seemingly happy for him, Aneesh was lost somewhere in his own thoughts.

'Congratulations, yaar. I am so happy for you.' Rajat, Aneesh's close friend and the director of Strategy in the same company hugged Aneesh and gave him a pat on back. 'Best Director! Haan.' He smiled making Aneesh stretch his lips to form a fake smile.

'Thank you, Rajat.'

'You must be a happy man, yaar. The title of "best director" doesn't come to everyone so easily. You have really worked hard for it. I am so proud of you. Your family must be so happy hearing this news.' Rajat cheerfully hugged him once again.

'Family? Did Rajat just say that?' Aneesh pondered.

This word—'family'—had lost its true sense for him in the past few years.

'Haan, yaar,' he replied rather meekly. 'But I don't share my achievements with my family. Barkha doesn't take them well. She always had the habit of comparing me with others. Moreover, she feels insecure if I tell her about my success stories. To her, I am good for nothing. So basically you see how lonely I am.'

'Leave it, yaar. I know how Barkha bhabhi is. But today is your day and we need to celebrate it. Just forget the rest!'

Making a deliberate attempt to cheer his friend up, Rajat dragged Aneesh to the parking lot and he reluctantly followed. Aneesh took out the keys of his Honda City and smiled at Rajat.

'That's like a good man!' Rajat exclaimed.

Getting into the car, they both decided to buy some liquor and sit quietly in a restaurant. Out of many attractions that Gurgaon as a city had to offer, BYOB was one of them. BYOB meant 'bring your own booze.' The BYOB locations were the most preferred ones in the city for folks who wished to unwind with a pint after a long day at work.

The duo left Signature Tower, the building that housed their office, soon after they decided on a place to go to. Rajat had suggested Lake Forest Wines, to which Aneesh had willingly agreed. After all, it was only peace of mind that he needed, rest everything else was secondary.

∾

It was 6.00 p.m. when they left for their destination. The giant of a city seemed too melodramatic at night. The city was filled with pragmatic energy from within. The shiny glass buildings, the large number of commuters, the swanky malls, the liquor bars, the lights, the glittery roads, all added to its charm. The streets were crowded and everyone seemed to be in a rush. Whether the people were on their way back home, or to a beer shop like him, Aneesh had no idea.

Crawling along in the heavy traffic with sirens and horns beeping all around, they took a halt at a red light. There was silence in the car, except for an old melody that played on the radio when Rajat suddenly exclaimed, 'People in Gurgaon have so much money, dude. Money flows like anything. You can see that here. There are so many attractions on the road… Mercedes-Benz C-Class, Mercedes-Benz S-Class, Audi, Land Rover. See…' He turned to Aneesh, 'Twelve Mercedes, eight Audis, ten Land Rovers and four Jaguars in just five minutes.'

Aneesh smiled and twisted his car keys. The signal had turned green. 'Leave na, yaar. There is no point in counting the cars or even any of such materialistic things. They do not guarantee you real happiness and happiness is not a puppet in the hands of such worldly pleasures.'

Rajat smiled back. They both looked at each other and then out of the window. The car inched its way through the busy streets till they reached Lake Forest Wines. Steadily making their way towards the beer shop, Rajat exclaimed, 'Let me show you something!'

Aneesh remained silent. He knew the conversation that would follow. Rajat screamed at the salesman to fetch him some really expensive wines and he smiled back at him in return.

'See this?' Holding a bottle of whiskey with both his hands, Rajat turned to Aneesh, who was by then fiddling with his phone. '₹50,000 ki whiskey! I have also had champagne priced at ₹1,00,000.'

There was a hint of pride in his words.

'Take it, yaar, whichever you want to and just tell me the amount to pay.' Aneesh was disinterested in Rajat's one-sided conversation. He pondered about the world where even liquor was a thing to show off.

'Monkey Shoulder, Glenfiddich, Laphroaig…' Rajat murmured as he got hold of the wine bottles and steadily made his way out of the liquor shop with Aneesh.

'Which way to now?' Aneesh asked as they both took their seats in the car.

Rajat kept the bottles at the back seat and turned to him. 'The Friends Republic. What say?'

'Nice one!' Aneesh agreed.

Driving cautiously through the crowded street, they reached The Friends Republic. A BYOB place, The Friends Republic was a super fancy and cool hangout. The shack-like ambiance with lip-smacking nibbles and upbeat music added to its charm. They both took a seat somewhere in the corner and Rajat placed the liquor on the table.

'How are your children, Rajat? Did you see them in the past few months?' Aneesh inquired.

If he had a secret, his friend too had one that needed to be blurted out.

'No,' Rajat replied in dismay, gulping down a glass of wine.

Guzzling a few more drinks, Rajat felt a lot light-headed. Aneesh kept staring at him, who deliberately made shots to overcome his side of unhappiness that ruled over him.

'I love Rhea. I still love her. She is my wife and the mother of my children. I still love her, though she may choose to avoid me,' Rajat murmured softly, feeling tipsy all over.

It is truly said that wine brings to light the hidden secrets of the soul. This is exactly what was happening with Rajat. He was pouring out his deepest secrets willfully in front of Aneesh, who chose to remain silent.

'I miss my children, yaar. They are my life,' Rajat blurted out. 'We were in love. Who would have thought such a thing would happen in a love marriage? This was our decision and we were so happy with it until Rhea's mother stepped in and ruined it all. She has total control over Rhea. It's been six months since I saw her or our children. She has even filed for a divorce. What to do, yaar! Sometimes, life gives us such shit!'

'Then why do you count so much on these materialistic things when you do not have that peace of mind? Real happiness comes from within, and not from all these worldly pleasures. They do not offer comfort for long. As long as we men get emotional support, we are okay, and trust me that true love is more important than all this. Rest is just an eyewash,' Aneesh consoled Rajat who held his head low in solitude.

'Accha, tell me, Rajat,' Aneesh continued. 'You have so many girlfriends. You are so popular in office and you were the one to tell me that they gifted you costly items for your new flat. Ruchi gifted you a sofa, Seema gave you a dining table...'

'Dude, these girls are good for nothing. It's all a mere show-off. They are not after me, but my power and position. They are doing this because they need a good appraisal from me this year. I throw parties almost every weekend and these are all in want of that stardust. Nothing else!' Rajat confessed.

The wine was working.

'Moreover, in this women-dominated world, if you talk to a girl about women's liberation and curse a man, she will be ready to sleep with you. You just need to talk to them in their favour. They cannot complete anyone because they themselves break their family.' Rajat's anguish was gradually becoming more and more intense with every word that he spoke. 'Family is family. Nothing can replace it. I miss my wife and children very much. Anyways, you tell me. What's with Barkha bhabhi?'

Now it was Aneesh's turn to blurt out the deep agony that he had suppressed for so long. It was not something to fight over with his wife. It was beyond a trivial fight.

'What's there to say, yaar? You already know it all. She is a self-sufficient lady who doesn't need me.' Aneesh kept his head lowered all the while.

'Why do you say so? Can't things be worked out between the two of you?' questioned Rajat, feeling extremely sorry for his friend.

'I don't think so. The more I need her and try to explain things, the more she distances herself, making me feel guilty for everything. She knows only this much,' Aneesh replied with dismay.

'Why don't you talk to her once and for all?' Rajat suggested.

'It's useless to talk to her, for every word that I'll say, she'll contradict with her absurd reasons,' Aneesh replied. 'And then about sex. She would bribe me with it to get whatever she wants and would withhold it if I fail to succumb. Experiencing the pleasure once, we men yearn for more and she knows that. Not only this, she knows how to withdraw it and then blame me for even the slightest mistake.'

'So you always seem to be at the receiving end.'

Aneesh let out a long weary sigh as he replied, 'Unfortunately, yes. She never seems to need me as she is the epitome of self-sufficiency. At least she thinks that way. There is no two-sided conversation between us. It's only one-sided and that's hers. I feel pissed off when I see my children being fed by their mother in a world-winning manner. It's all about "the best" for her. She has never learnt to compromise. The concept of "average" never works for her. Either it's the best or nothing.'

Rajat didn't know how to console his friend, so he chose to listen patiently while Aneesh dolefully continued with his words.

'She blames me for everything. It seems I am the only one who's 100 per cent responsible for every damn problem that crops up between us. For her, I am just a loser who doesn't know how to take care of his family. I cannot fulfill her never-ending demands. Her needs have always been more than my pockets can cater to.'

'And your children?' Rajat questioned softly.

'They are always in favour of their mother, for she brought up them like that. There's no one in that building whom I can call my own. My ideas and suggestions never find a place there and I simply have a corner to myself.'

As they took sips of their drinks, Aneesh felt engulfed in the tragedy of his long-lost love life. The same was with Rajat, who kept thinking about Aneesh's words. There was a gap gradually created in their respective married lives. The thoughts of competing egos and aspirations, an empty marriage and finances, all filled up Aneesh's mind in a short span of time. He wondered if what Rajat said was true about people having half-night stands. It was easy to go to bed with someone. There are no strings attached and you even get a sort of mental satisfaction out of it. But was this one-night stand really a solution for people who use sex to get their mind off loneliness? Do people get their jollies by indulging in such acts? Does life have a more intimate and deeper meaning for these people?

The evening was getting more and more intense. Ironically, the worst pain always followed the best of drinks.

ల

'Come, Nivedita. You are here with your mom for the first time. Nice!' A plump lady in red caught hold of Nivedita, who stood beside her mother, feeling exhausted because of her tiring schedules. Her mother had insisted on her joining her for a kitty party and there she was...feeling awkward in a place where she barely knew anyone. Barkha nudged her and even scorned when she made faces out of rage.

'Go, join everyone. You'll feel good!' Barkha insisted

and let go of her hands.

The poor thing was never meant to join this kitty thing. She could have relaxed at home and surfed her favourite channels.

'Come na!' the lady—addressed by everyone as Mrs Dixit—caught hold of Nivedita's hand and began introducing her to the other ladies of the group. 'See. This is what life is!' she exclaimed.

Nivedita was least interested in them. As she sat staring at the high walls of the ostentatious hall of the Park Plaza, the ladies around her got busy with the show-off of their designer outfits and imported jewelleries.

'Oh my god! This neckpiece, Barkha! It seems so costly. From where did you buy it?'

'I went to Spain last weekend. This is just a small purchase.' Barkha smirked at the lady, who looked at her in awe.

'Even I went for an international holiday last month. My husband, you know. He's a travel freak and loves to travel around a lot. I am so tired of these international holidays now. It's kind of a normal routine, you see. Every month!' Mrs Dixit, no less an exhibitionist herself, was quick to respond to Barkha's Spain reply.

Everyone turned around to look at Mrs Dixit and asked in unison, 'Like really?'

'Oh, yes! I have told him a million times not to spend that much, but he says if we have it, why not spend it?' Mrs Dixit replied, pride evident in her eyes.

'I am not dependent on my husband for anything. I can travel and spend as much as I want and the way I want to.

You see, independent life.' A fake smile appeared on the lips of Mrs Aneesh Malhotra as she stole the attention of the ladies.

Mrs Dixit seemed crossed. 'So, Nivedita. What do you wish for in future? Expensive outfits, jewelleries, fancy cars, big bungalows or what?' she changed the topic in order to hide the annoyance that had by then overpowered her.

'Not sure…' Nivedita managed to utter. She had actually not dreamt of all this that was mentioned.

'She is preparing for her IIT exams. I want her to be independent, just like me and get the best out of life, *just like me*,' Barkha replied.

Nivedita seemed thankful and exchanged smiles with her mother.

'Very good!' Mrs Gupta of the kitty group exclaimed. 'We ladies should never be dependent on these men. They are just good for nothing. You should always control them if you want to live a carefree life.'

The other ladies laughed.

'Actually, Mrs Gupta, I would say "training" would be the word here,' Barkha muttered. 'Actually training a man is like training a dog. You have to use rewards and punishments to bend him to your will. If you stand your ground, he'll be eating out of your hand in just a few weeks. I guarantee.'

The hall was filled with fits of laughter. Barkha held her head high in consideration of her intelligence.

'True. If you have to live peacefully, you have to tame them. Just manipulate him with your cooking and silaai-karhaai (embroidery) skills and he will fall head over heels for you. This is just one of the ways we have. There are actually thirty-nine others.' Mrs Gupta smirked. She nudged the lady next to her who replied, '*Aadmi ko kabu karne ke chalees upay* (Forty ways to tame your man).'

Laughter filled the hall.

'These men will be men! They are one and the same and they do fall for these tricks again and again.'

'Nivedita beta, learn them. You'll also have to use them some day or the other.' Mrs Dixit pinched poor Nivedita on the elbow and she shrieked. '*Abhi se seekh lo. Baad me mauka nai milega* (Learn now. Later you will not get the opportunity).'

'Accha, ladies, what will you have? We need to place our orders also,' Barkha said, glancing at her watch.

'I'll have some Chinese and a pina colada,' said Mrs Dixit.

Mrs Gupta placed her order for a green apple drink.

'And I'll go with some lemonade. I am on a diet.' Barkha completed the order summary and the waiter carefully jotted it down and left.

'Diet haan? You need some real extra effort to maintain this figure, Barkha?'

'Yes, of course. This comes handy when you really need to cut off your man. Give him sex once and next when you need something, and if he doesn't agree, just refuse. He'll come drooling and say yes.' Barkha winked at the lady sitting next to her.

'Ahaan! Nice tricks,' she replied.

'I sometimes don't talk to my husband if he does anything displeasing. You know what, men don't notice when it's all okay, but they are quick to notice when it's not,' Mrs Dixit chuckled. 'My husband is never interested in anything I say on a daily basis, but when I show him that I am upset, like if I stop talking to him, he usually asks, "*Kya hua*?" (What happened)and sometimes it feels so good to make him feel guilty for something he has no idea about.'

'Yes. That's so true!' Mrs Gupta guffawed at the remark. 'If my man doesn't agree for a shopping spree, something that I like the most, I usually pretend to be disinterested in all his tasks. And even if he tries to start a conversation, I pretend to be busy. That's the perfect way to bring him back on line.'

'You know what, friends, I have made this habit of praising myself in front of him every time he is in a good mood. That way he remembers it even if we have a fight. It's nice to show him your puppy face and he falls for it every time.'

'That's even nicer!' the lady replied back with a grin.

'And what if your husband still doesn't surrender to your fancies?' another lady in their group questioned with a raised brow.

'Then, simple…' Barkha took over the charge next. 'Tell him, you'll go to your mom's house or use your children to protect you in front of their dads. Believe me, this thing always works,' she whispered. 'You can also stop talking to him, ladies. You know, act like the desi-aurat type. Make him feel guilty for destroying world peace. This thing has worked for me a trillion times actually!'

'Stop it now. We are being quite bitchy,' Mrs Dixit smiled and raised a toast to the kitty ladies.

'And men love bitches!' winked Barkha.

ꟷ

There was loads of laughter, food, drinks and gossips that related mainly with *How to train men and bring them on track.*

Actually every woman wants to be loved. She wants to progress from being a doormat to a dream girl. And she wants to have some autonomy or control over her life, if not his. In short, she wants to know how to win men over, how to control them and how to have them for keeps. It could be a *seedhi-sadhi* type *in a lawn ka three-piece salwar kameez* or a woman in a palazzo and a tee, stepping out of a coffee shop. At the end of the day, the same predictable techniques work.

The grown-up version of theory comes into play when a woman is unsatisfied with some aspect of the man in her life. She then starts to openly make unflattering comparisons between other people and her man. Such statements not only shame a man, but they also prey on his ego. Being very hard to please and holding grudges are two other things they start doing. Right out of these Ekta Kapoor serials, you know. Somewhere, it's all about resorting to the Star Plus methods of dominance and believe me, these prove that something is seriously wrong somewhere.

Thus, at the kitty party, over some really expensive food, some really narrow-minded conversations followed. At the end of the day, where emotions were being drained out at one end, they were also being stomped on the other. Relationships have always been a tricky affair and will be so *ALWAYS*!

5

Meditation: Rites de Passage of the Rich

It was a quiet Sunday morning. There were four people in the white Xcent, including the chauffeur. The coldness outside matched the mood inside the four-wheeler. None of them spoke as the vehicle steadily made its way towards the massive meditation centre located on the outskirts of the city. As the driver took a right turn near IIM Lucknow, Aradhya rolled down the window. The cold wind blew against her face as she tried hard to shrug off the thoughts of her past. Just as she was about to turn around, she felt a soft hand over her hands.

'You should settle down with someone after your daughters are married,' Aradhya's mother looked at her, trying to put some sense into her daughter, just like she had been for years now after Ravi's demise.

Ravi was Aradhya's late husband and a brave army officer. He was the epitome of an ideal man. But, it had been years now since his demise and Aradhya had two daughters to take care of. Aradhya's mother, Mrs Anjana—just the way mothers are—was concerned for her daughter and her loveless life after Ravi. Aradhya had been listening to all of this for a very long time.

'Hmm…' she replied, her gesture displayed to all what her mother had to offer.

It was not that she didn't feel aloof or that she didn't miss Ravi, but she had learnt to move on in life and her only dream now was to bring up her two daughters in the best possible way. Just the way Ravi would have done.

After eleven years of her fairy-tale marriage, the sudden storm of Ravi's demise had torn her apart and her inner self knew how difficult it had been for her to raise two beautiful daughters all by herself. She had managed to tie the strings of her life well. To fill up the emptiness, she had become a member of the Ram Krishna Mission. Meditation was what she used as a tool to find inner solace.

She closed her eyes and let the cool wind caress her face once again. 'Marriage is surely not in my cards right now,' she thought, looking out of the window.

ര

The parking lot at the meditation centre was occupied with a large number of expensive cars along with blue-beaconed ambassadors, parked right next to them. Uniformed guards stood in full attention, guarding their masters' possessions. It seemed the richer or better known these people were, the more peace they craved for. Else, there would have been no need for these starry folks to be in a place like a meditation centre! If only life was as wonderful as it seemed!

'Stop here. *Yahin rok do*, Ram Singh,' Aradhya gestured

the driver to stop the car as soon as he found a good parking spot in the premises. Fidgeting through her handbag, she took out her phone and dialled a number.

'Hello, Mumma,' the voice at the other end was filled with affection. It was her daughter.

'Nandu beta, I have reached and I am going to switch off my cell phone now. I'll switch it on as soon as the session is over.'

'Okay, Mumma. Take care. We'll wait for you.'

'You too, beta. I'll be home soon.'

'Bye, Mumma!'

'Bring the car here after the meditation is over,' Aradhya murmured to the driver as she kept her phone in the small handbag slung over her frail shoulders.

'Ji, madam!' came the reply instantly.

*

Aradhya took a seat at one corner of the room, with her mother seated beside her. She felt she was late for the session, as only a handful of seats were left by the time she had reached. Looking around the large hall and the people seated inside, one could easily figure out that life outside was indeed just a show-off for them. It was way different from what they actually showed it to be. Shimmery from the outside and hollow from within. That was the reason maybe, why the rich segments of society, including the top bureaucrats were lined up here, or maybe they were there to run away from their concealed identities, or maybe it was just a ritual required to wash away their sins—just like bathing in the holy Ganges. The meditation centre offered all of it!

∾

It was fifteen minutes since Aradhya and her parents were inside. Ram Singh was pacing up and down the lane when he overheard a conversation some other drivers were having. It sounded interesting to him and he was tempted to join in. There was a driver dressed smartly in police-like uniform, along with a gunner. Upon inquiring, he came to know their names, Sonu and Rahul. There was another chauffeur named Suresh. Introducing himself to the the group, Ram Singh joined in too.

'It's a busy day today. Both Sa'ab and Mem sa'ab have a long schedule ahead of them. From here, they will go for a movie in Fun Cinemas. That new one... What was the name? Ummm...*Ae Dil Hai Mushkil*, yes that one. Then Madam will go to her kitty party at Renaissance and Sirji has to go clubbing with his friends. This means not a single minute of rest for me today,' Sonu, the driver in the smart uniform, remarked, disheartened. He had planned an outing with his family, but it seemed he wasn't going to get enough time for it. Poor chap!

'These big people have their own tantrums. All of this meditation is a mere show-off. It is more like a ritual for them. Come every Sunday and they try to get rid of all your misdeeds. Once a week is enough to show off morality,' Rahul commented. 'Our meditation is complete the day we manage to have two meals. When I see my children sleeping with a full stomach, I feel relieved. At least, this is what the life of a poor man is.'

'Happiness and sorrow all come from within,' Suresh

added. 'We don't have time for such rituals. Our whole day is busy arranging for food for the entire family.' There was a tint of sadness in his eyes.

Ironically, the people who have it all are deprived of the basic ingredient for a happy life—peace, and the ones who have in abundance this five-letter thing never ever have *it all!* How true!

'This meditation and all, I guess is what my sa'ab ji, who is a big name in the homeopathy field, calls placebo,' Suresh said.

Meanwhile, Ram Singh was listening to all of the conversation. At least it was making some sense, unlike some of the conversations he had with rich people. He could relate to it.

'What is a placebo?' Sonu inquired.

'It is a procedure prescribed for the psychological benefit of the patient rather than for any physiological effect,' Suresh answered. 'It is a sort of treatment used to deceive the patient into thinking that it is an active treatment. It is mainly used when the recipient perceives an improvement in condition due to personal expectations, rather than the treatment itself,' he further explained.

'Oh!' the others exclaimed. It was a new concept for them.

'Likewise. This medication is like a placebo for these people where they are made to believe that they are cleansing their entire self in just an hour! This works well for them.'

'You are absolutely right. The more you have, the more distant you are from a peaceful sleep.'

'Do you know…' It was Ram Singh's turn to put forth his views. Listening to everyone, he suddenly felt an urge to speak up. 'The compound of this centre has a "plotting system" also. You need to be a member of this mission to be able to own a plot here. And do you know how costly these plots are? What I feel is that this center and all this is just a way to promote their plotting system. More the people become their members, the better it will be for the authorities. Isn't it?

'Exactly! Actually it works just like an Amway system. First you become a member, then in order to get the benefits, you need to make others a member too. And this goes on. It's a long chain.'

'True. This is all a marketing strategy of the richer segments. Nothing to do with us people,' Rahul said with a nod.

'Have you seen the master trainer's room?' Sonu stepped in this time. 'It's breathtakingly beautiful. What comfort! Full AC! Sometimes I think of quitting this chauffeur's job and becoming a saint. What luxury these people have!'

'I agree! They have all the worldly pleasures we can think of.'

Suddenly, there was a hustle at some distance that made everyone stand erect.

'Chalo, chalo! Let's go. Let's wrap up our satsang. Our masters will be here any moment. Let's move now and fetch the cars,' said Ram Singh and everyone dispersed in haste. 'What a conversation it was!' he thought.

∾

Aradhya and her parents went back home after the ritual of the early Sunday morning. Life had been hard on Aradhya. She had successfully raised her two daughters, facing all the hardships of being a single mother. She had stayed with her parents after Ravi's demise and looked after them also. They had always supported her well in this new life. Working in a competitive company that was into Training and Development, Aradhya had also persistently met her career demands over the long run. She was into everything and everything had been her priority. But all this had never been easy. The transformation from being an ideal wife and a beta woman to an alpha female had eventually changed the life that she lived! And her family was proud of it all!

What was lacking in her life was Ravi's presence and she secretly missed him every day. Even after his demise, her family admired him. Others were endlessly compared to him and his memories were brought into conversations almost every other day.

When Aradhya and her parents reached home, their maid was busy preparing breakfast for the kids. Aradhya called everyone as she laid the breakfast on the table. Her mother helped her out with the servings. The daughters were delighted to have everyone back at home, but it seemed they were cross with each other over something and Aradhya soon figured it out, thanks to her sixth sense.

'What is it? The two of you seem upset,' she asked, passing a plate to Simran, the younger of the two.

'Mummy, Simran makes the room a mess. She eats on the bed and leaves the leftovers there. The room stinks,' Nandu complained.

Aradhya was right in guessing that something was cooking between the two.

'So? What is wrong with eating on the bed? I don't get

it. I'll eat where I want to,' Simran retorted.

'I have to light up an incense stick to remove the smell,' Nandu continued to protest.

'You do whatever you like and I'll do whatever I like.'

'Okay! Stop fighting you two and have your breakfast quietly.' Aradhya had to step before it turned into a catfight.

The children took their plates and finished their breakfast in silence, not missing out any opportunity to pass an angry look at the other.

The elders watched away amused, reliving the past and remembering the fights between Aradhya and her younger sister over trivial matters. 'Our Aradhya has grown up!' they thought, exchanging glances. There was silence for a while when Mr Chauhan, Aradhya's father decided to break the ice.

'I need to pay Mr Pawan, your uncle, a visit today in the hospital. He is admitted to SGPGI for kidney ailments. I got a call from their family last night. I think I'll be going with Arun this afternoon…'

'Why Arun?' Aradhya interrupted, taking a small bite of her corn sandwich. 'I'll drop you there, Papa.'

'No, beta. You take some rest. Only one day you get to rest your body and mind. The other days you are extremely busy with your chores. Moreover, the extra workload that you take these days has triggered your spondylitis pain. I'll go with Arun,' her father insisted.

'You don't want to go out with me because I am a girl?'

'No. It's nothing like that. Just that Arun told me he too needs to go there.'

'Hmm… Okay, Papa. You go with him if you think it's all right,' Aradhya conceded as she took a tissue and wiped her mouth.

Aradhya was indeed very lucky to have a family that had supported her well during all the troubled times—be it emotionally or otherwise. Her parents always provided her with the companionship that she craved for after Ravi. It had been the end of a fairy-tale married life when she heard the unexpected news and her world fell apart. A perfect and idealistic marriage is what she had shared with him, never ever caring to look outside, not even behind the four walls of her home. In all these years, she had tried to negotiate well with the outside world and had come up on her own terms. She was happy and confident now. Driving was a new passion for her; it gave her 'control kicks', just the way she had controlled her life.

Her children and her parents were an important part of her life and she had to take care of them. After her husband, she had taken utmost care to nurture them well. Being rooted to the belief that she had to do anything and everything for her daughters, Aradhya had managed to give them all that they needed for a comfortable life. It was like she had boycotted her own life for the sake of her family. Just the way Ravi would have. She never wanted her children to grow up missing their father and thinking that life would have been different if he were alive. What was missing was authority and guidance in her parenting. She was too conscious of what people would say rather than what was good for the children. And this had made her go beyond rationality to succumb to the demands of her family. Over years, she had gradually turned from a perfect homemaker to a narcissist independent working women.

6

I Surrender at First Sight: You Fight

Holding up her cup of hot chocolate, Aradhya glanced at her watch. It was 5 p.m. It had been quite some time since she had arrived and now it felt like a coon's age to her. It was almost half an hour past their mutually decided time to meet. She decided to leave the place when her phone rang.

'Hello,' she answered.

'I am so sorry, Aradhya. You had to wait. Well I am outside now. Where are you?' a familiar voice on the other end greeted Aradhya and she felt a bit relaxed. 'Finally!' she thought. It was Barkha. She was in town and the duo had decided to meet in the evening in the posh locality of Gomti Nagar. Renaissance was the place that they had mutually decided to meet at after much consideration.

'I am waiting for you in the lobby area. Come over,' Aradhya replied.

'Okay! Just give me a minute.'

It was after ages that the two were going to be face to face with each other, leaving apart the brief meeting at the formal award function.

'Hey, Aradhya!' Dressed in a crisp white shirt and a low-waist trouser, and a waistcoat held casually in her hands, Barkha looked like a proficient young lady. She smiled at Aradhya, who hugged her back.

'I am so sorry for being late. Was stuck with some important work.'

'Oh! Never mind. I came in just a while ago,' Aradhya lied. 'So tell me, what would you like to have?'

'A glass of water, to be honest. I am dying of thirst!' Barkha replied promptly.

'So, what brought you here today? Office work?' Aradhya inquired.

'Yeah! I had a meeting with an important client in Hazratganj. Was stuck there only. You tell me. How is life? It's been long since we met? College days and this day. A lot has changed, na?'

'Right! Life has been a roller coaster all this while. You have kids?'

'Yes, two. And you?'

'Two daughters.'

'What are they doing currently?'

'Oh! The elder one, Simran, has joined the Pearl Institute for a fashion course and the younger one, Nandu, is in grade tenth. She is in Loreto.'

'That's nice and that makes us equally pissed. The children and family, argh!' Barkha said with a grin.

'I guess that makes us equally responsible!' Aradhya replied. 'So what's up at your end?'

'Actually nothing worth talking about, apart from my work. I have a dull husband and kids to look after. His

become shit with him. Tell me about yourself. I heard you got married to an army officer. Isn't it?'

'Yes.' A smile escaped Aradhya's lips as she answered. Her eyes sparkled as she reminisced about the beautiful past she had. 'His name was Ravi.'

'Was?'

'Hmm… He is no more.' All of a sudden, her eyes lost their shine. 'He lost his life years back. It was a major heart attack.'

'Oh! I am so sorry.'

'No, don't be,' replied Aradhya. 'I don't want anyone to feel sorry for me. In fact, I am really proud of what he was and will always be. Yes, life is at times dull without him and I do miss him, but I am okay now. He has left a beautiful past for me to cherish and I slip into it whenever I feel aloof.'

'Oh! Lucky you! You had a husband like that. With Aneesh, I don't feel any of it.'

'But you yourself chose him over your ex.'

'Yes. But that was because I didn't feel there could be a secure future with him.'

'So why regret now? It was a non-coercive decision.'

'You are right. But I could have someone better than Aneesh. It seems I never took enough time to decide. My bad. Anyways, so how did your love story begin?'

'Well, it started when Papa was posted in Kanpur and I had completed my MSc Botany course. Like any other girl, I also had suitors and proposals.'

Barkha listened silently, looking at Aradhya, who blushed like an adolescent.

'Someone told my father about Ravi. He was then an army captain of repute and his family lived in Ludhiana. Papa was at once interested in him and so he sent my photograph along with the biodata to his parents.'

'Then?'

'After a few days, we received a call from them saying that they liked my proposal and his mother wanted to personally meet me.'

'Oh... The typical Indian types. Chai-shai...'

Aradhya smiled. 'Yes. His parents came all the way from Ludhiana to meet me. They finalized everything but his father had only one condition, "Let Ravi come and let the two meet".'

'So what did you or your parents say?'

'There was no problem on our part either. We were okay with it and I was happy to get a chance to meet him.'

'Ahaan... Carry on.'

'Ravi came two months later. It was his break. We met. I was completely bowled over by his etiquettes and mannerism. He was perfect. He treated me like a lady, just as a gentleman would. He told me about his salary. It was not much. Just 25k at that time! Moreover, they also had the liability of a loan that they had taken over his PF and it was being continuously deducted from his pay.'

'Oh... Then? You should have refused to marry him without a minute's delay. That was quite a low pay,' Barkha said.

'Yes, it was. But I liked him as a whole. Money was never a problem and it never will be. What mattered was the way he treated me, and his true and genuine confessions.

I sort of liked it and I am happy I made a right decision. No regrets.'

'Okay. So?'

'I was eager to hear all that he had to say. He told me about his life in the army. There were so many stringent rules attached to his life there. But with him, I was ready to face it all. It was as if, with him, I had an emotional string attached. Families, as he told me were not allowed in the field postings and his posting was soon to be in the Jammu region, where supposedly we wouldn't be allowed.'

'It sounds tough for a newlywed,' Barkha said with her eyebrows raised at the display of such devotion.

'Yes, it was.'

'What happened then?'

'There was an emotional whirlwind inside me all the time. I along with him and a few of my friends also went to a bird sanctuary. I was happy that he behaved well with all of them. Actually another gesture of his won me over. You know what? Ravi was a non-vegetarian and I a typical vegetarian. Once, we went out for dinner in Meghdoot. He offered me a chicken dish.'

'Don't tell me you gave in to his fancies and tasted it.'

'Yes. I did. Because he was nice to me and as I said, I had started to like him...a lot, in fact!'

'That means you surrendered then and there,' Barkha remarked, making her usual that-was-not-acceptable face.

'No, it was actually a gesture that said I was ready to face this new life with him...together!'

'Oh! What a gesture indeed...' Barkha seemed to be in total disagreement with what Aradhya was saying. Giving up and that too so easily, from the first instance itself was not her thing. 'Go ahead...'

'Ravi's mother even took us to Parmat in the morning, the very next day. Though there was a huge crowd there, with Ravi near me, everything else had ceased to matter. He took care of me and his mother all the while, till we were safe outside. For the first time in my life, I felt so secure and like I belonged. It seemed as if life had gradually begun to change, for good!' Aradhya smiled, glowing all the while she talked about Ravi and her life with him.

'When he took me out to Kwality Restaurant was the best day. We had apple juice and ice cream, and of course, a long conversation. He gifted me a gajra the same day from Moti jheel. It was on our way back home. He wanted me to dress up in a saree and like an obedient person, I abided. He was so happy and I was too. Actually, it felt good seeing him happy about a thing that I did for him.'

Barkha remained silent. She had nothing of that sort to share. Her marriage with Aneesh had been troublesome since the very beginning. She deliberately chose to keep her lips sealed all the while Aradhya spoke.

'The next day Ravi left,' Aradhya continued. 'A week's later date was fixed by everyone for our engagement. Engagement! This word brought a spark in my life and I remember being all happy on hearing the news. Family members were informed and there was a lot of preparation. The following week, we went to Ludhiana for the rituals. There were so many calculations going on in my mind at that time. There were tussles and immediate solutions too.

Everything was going to change, but I was happily okay with all of it.'

'Hmm… So you got engaged in Ludhiana.'

'Yeah! An air force station at Ludhiana was the venue for the engagement. At that time, I didn't know how to wear a saree.' Aradhya blushed. 'My sister-in-law draped it for me. His family members, especially all the ladies, teased us. Even the male members pulled Ravi's leg. We were shy to initiate a conversation in front of so many guests. But our eyes said it all. Amidst a lot of joking around and applause, we exchanged rings. There was a silent, unsaid promise to be with each other, no matter what!' Aradhya's eyes went teary as she uttered those last words.

Barkha, who was listening intently, passed Aradhya a tissue and she wiped the drops of tears that slid down her eye.

'After a courtship of around four months, with Ravi and me meeting occasionally, the date of our wedding was fixed. Once, in between he had come to Delhi on some official purpose and I remember leaving my city with a friend to meet him. At that time, Papa was posted in Meerut and we stayed in the circuit house. It was fun and luckily, nothing went wrong. Ravi took good care of us.'

Barkha smiled. For the first time in the entire conversation, she found a reason to. Her relation with Aneesh had been way different. There had always been a chaotic phase since their marriage. Yes, before marriage, when they were in a relationship, it was good but post marriage, life was quite troubled.

'What would you like to have, ma'am?' the waiter's voice suddenly interrupted her thoughts. 'One pina colada for me.

And you?' Barkha asked, turning to Aradhya.

'One fresh lime mojito and spring rolls.'

'Veg or non-veg?' the waiter asked in a soft voice.

'Veg.'

'Sure, ma'am.' He carefully penned down the order and left.

'Are you sure you don't want to eat anything else?' Barkha turned to Aradhya, who was busy fidgeting with her phone for a perfect selfie click. 'No! I am full. Tell me more about your relationship with Aneesh,' she replied turning her phone upside down.

'Oh, he's actually an authoritarian. Though he himself is just good for nothing, but he behaves like a boss all the time and expects me to obey his decisions. From my children's education to their choice of colleges and now their careers, it's like I am the only one who is responsible for everything. Aneesh doesn't even know what is best for them, or for me, or even for himself. He's so impractical and so immature at times, I just cannot explain. All I can tell you is that I am in a very pathetic married life right now. There is no way out.'

'It's sad to hear that. What about your children?' Aradhya questioned.

'Of course they are my side. Why will they listen to a good-for-nothing father who knows nothing about their future?' Barkha retorted. 'I keep on telling Nivedita about things that she needs to take care of when she gets married. You know, life can turn into a disaster if you give in to your husband's whims and fancies. After my work, I try and spend time outside the house. You see there is no point getting into frequent conflicts with Aneesh over every trivial matter.'

'I agree.' Aradhya nodded dolefully.

'Anyways, you continue with your story. What did Ravi tell you abou this army life? Was it easy?'

'No. It had never been easy for me. Coming from an independent background, I felt caged at first,' Aradhya replied, her voice curt.

'I agree. You are bound to feel that way.'

'Hmm... But after a certain time, I got used to it all. In fact, when I look back today, I count myself lucky for having been exposed to that kind of life.'

'In spite of so many rules and regulations?'

'Yes. I gradually learnt to transform my frivolous college-girl attitude into that of an army officer's wife. Ravi, needless to say, helped me out with everything. He remained my pillar of strength throughout the transformation process.'

'Yes, but that's because he wanted you to change. Men will be men!'

'No. It was all because I wanted to change. I had started to like it all. I learnt to mix with people from different backgrounds. Yes, it was tough to be a part of the army life but truly speaking, that life has its own charm. The army is one establishment where one's social etiquette is honed to perfection. There are so many gatherings and you just cannot stay away from them. Honestly, I never even wanted to.' Aradhya took a pause and gulped down a glass of water kept near her. In all these years, she had never shared this much with anyone. It seemed all her emotions were bottled-up till she met Barkha.

'Carry on,' Barkha said placing a hand on Aradhya's.

She felt good.

'On 20 November, we got married and after a few years, I got pregnant with our first child. Initially, I didn't even know how to cook, but I learned. It was a good time. He helped me out with everything and never complained. I couldn't join a 9–5 job because of the new life. The whole day seemed to be an endless wait, waiting for Ravi to return. But then, I do not regret it also. Yes, there were times when the loneliness stretched, especially when Ravi was away for temporary duty or exercise sessions. But then, the ladies rallied around to support each other as a family.'

'So, you never felt the need of your family? That's what you mean to say?'

'Of course, I did. But it was all like a new family for me—somewhere I could find solace when Ravi was not there. Actually the social commitments of an army wife are all encompassing, but it can be profoundly satisfying too, depending on the way you look at it.'

'I see…'

'Hmm. Had I not married an army man, so many creative arts would have bypassed me. At every posting, I loved the challenge of dressing up a new quarter to suit our needs.'

'Didn't all of this seem monotonous ever?'

'Oh, no! Never! In fact, it was always fun. Meeting different people at different places and then forming a family. There were so many things I learnt post marriage that I was unaware of. It was all like a new opportunity explored for the first time!'

'Huh! Opportunity? Without a job? Without a career?'

'Yes! It was an altogether different, yet nice experience.

Not exactly a career but nevertheless, not less than that also. I believe every woman has an artistic side to her personality. Just think, how many of them are lucky enough to explore it? From gardening to public speaking, I had the chance to master it all. Moreover, I learnt to behave like a lady. A quotient of elegance, you see! How many girls get a chance like that?'

'So, you mean you enjoyed it all?'

'Oh, yes! I did! Midnight picnics, a sudden outing, rain dances, beach parties, barbeques, dandia dances, disco parties, Halloween, festivals and everything I can remember, I cherished it all. For me, the pride I feel as an army officer's wife is worth all the sacrifices I have ever had to make. It's a badge of honour to be a part of such a beautiful family.'

Barkha's pina colada was left untouched. She was way too engrossed in hearing about Aradhya's life. 'So difficult a life she's had, yet she's so elegant,' she thought.

ര

'So, your ex… What was his name?' Aradhya asked, sipping her drink.

'Rahul. By the time he proposed to me, he had already cracked the civil service exam.'

'Oh! That's nice. At least he had a secure job in hand. So you left him for no reason?'

'A secure job? Don't you know that a government job doesn't pay that much if you want to live a luxurious life? Being simply settled with a plain "secure job" wasn't the thing that I wanted with a man. I had high ambitions and I don't think there's anything wrong with it.'

'No, there's nothing wrong. But sacrificing your love for…'

'Sacrificing? There's no such thing in life, Aradhya,' Barkha interrupted. 'I always got what I wanted. Or to put it straight, I always worked for what I wanted and I deserved the best, I guess.'

'At the cost of relationships?' Aradhya asked, raising a brow.

'There's nothing in this world that is free of cost, Aradhya, and I hope you know that.'

'Hmm…'

'But I never knew Aneesh would be like this. So boring he is! Our thoughts never match and we are poles apart. I like to have my own ways and who knows this better than you people.'

'Argh! Right! You haven't changed a bit.'

'Why should I? I mean I am perfect like this. I am an independent woman, Aradhya, and I don't like to walk on the path shown by others. In fact, I like to create my own. That's why I am here. The status, the power, the position, it's all because I have worked hard for it. Had I listened to Aneesh years back, I would have been a plain housewife with no dignity. Doing all the household chores and looking after the children would have been my ultimate aim. Is this what you call a life? You tell me. Being jobless and depending on the mercy of others. Well, I never wanted that and I am happy like this.'

Aradhya listened quietly. At least she agreed with Barkha on the point that it was necessary for a woman to be self-dependent, and who could have known this better than name is Aneesh and he is really not my type. Life would have been much better if I would have married my ex. Aneesh was my second choice, you see.'

'Ex?' Aradhya questioned, puzzled.

'Hmm. I left him for Aneesh. He was not well-to-do and I never wanted to marry a person like him in my life. A government job in hand wouldn't have ever satisfied my dreams. My dreams were big, like one's should be. But Aneesh is so irresponsible. Just the opposite. I feel caged at times.'

'Argh… I am sorry to hear that. And your kids?'

'Nivedita, my daughter, is trying for IIT. I wish she succeeds so that she doesn't ever have to settle for anything less in life. And my son, Ayaan, is still very young, but I have plans for him as well.'

'Your husband doesn't have a say?'

'Have a say? In what? He really is an empty-headed man. Not worthy at all. What will he say when he doesn't understand things himself? I don't want my children to grow up like their father.'

'A loser?' Aradhya was a bit taken aback.

How could a person who had set up a good, in fact a high living standard for his family be a loser. 'He must be a hardworking guy,' she thought. 'But I thought you have all the comforts in life. Isn't it so?' she asked.

'Yes. But that's all because of me. Had I not coaxed him into doing things, we wouldn't have been so well-to-do. He's such a jerk,' Barkha replied, wiping her face with a moisturizing tissue. She then crumpled the piece of tissue and aimed it at the trash bin kept at a distance. 'Life has her. Taking care of the kids after her husband's demise and facing the brutal world by her own to become a successful personality had not been easy for her.

'And I think my children should also get nothing but the best out of their life and I am training them in such a manner from the very beginning. I don't think it's a bad idea. Men will always demoralize you and dance on your head if you let them rule upon you. That's why I am surprised you gave in to Ravi so easily. He would never have understood your true value because you never showed that to him.'

'Umm... Actually I never had to face the real world when he was there. My world was confined to the four walls and I was pretty happy with it until he left...' There was a sudden pause. 'It was tough being a wife without a husband and being a single parent. There was a lot of criticism and boundaries laid for me. But I had to surpass them all, for the sake of my children.'

'Oh! So where are you nowadays?'

'At my parents' home. I have been there since that fateful day and I must say that I have been lucky to find comfort at their place. They took good care of me and my little ones. I couldn't have been able to achieve all this without their continuous support. Even today, they are my pillars of strength.'

'Don't you miss your husband?' Barkha inquired.

'Of course, I do. But I have the courage now to move on and I know my family will always be there for me, no matter what. They have helped me out during the most traumatic phase of my life. I have learnt to walk alone and with confidence in all these years. Ravi is a beautiful past that I'll always cherish, but I have to make a beautiful future for my children too. I have to give them all that their father would have if he were alive…' Aradhya paused for a minute. 'I couldn't fall asleep at night without going over every worst-case scenario that could befall my children and how to protect them from it. Believe me, Barkha, being both a father and a mother is never easy and you have a whole lot of responsibilities. I don't want the world to say, "*Papa hote inke to aisa hota.*" If they had a father, things would have been like this. I want it to be like "*Papa ke bina bhi aisa hai.*" Without a father also things are like this.'

There was a dreadful silence after that, which made Barkha fidget quite a number of times. After many years, Aradhya had let go of the pent-up emotions inside her. Barkha was speechless. She didn't know what to say. Of course, Aradhya didn't require any consolation. She had moved out of that phase long ago. Though her life was full of 'Oh, that was hard!' she had managed to keep going. Indeed the sheer amount of responsibilities she had juggled so far in all these years had made her a nurturer, caregiver, teacher, nurse, cheerleader, disciplinarian, and much more. During the hard times, she had constantly reminded herself that the reason for this precarious balancing act was to provide a better life to her kids. As far as Barkha was concerned, she realized that it was a supreme challenge for Aradhya. Her life tested her conviction and courage on a daily basis, and still she kept moving ahead. This is what life had actually taught her and brought her to a point where she no longer needed the sympathies of others.

'Accha, leave all this, past is past and I do not want to

sob over it during our entire meet,' Aradhya smiled back at Barkha, who was still finding it difficult to say anything. She smiled back in return.

ꟹ

'I was happy to see you at the award function that night,' Barkha initiated.

'Even I was. But we couldn't talk much that day.'

'Yeah! That was all because of the media and the people around, I guess,' replied Barkha. 'They need people like us and stories like ours to flaunt. The best celebrity being the one who gets the best coverage!'

'Hmm... Right! But then there were so many other people around you.'

'Yes! There were some who needed favours from me. You know my position, right? They knew I would help them out. Business, you know. I charge them for the favours. It's not charity that I do,' Barkha smirked.

'Oh! I should have understood,' Aradhya nodded her head.

'Leave it, yaar. This is normal routine. I am used to all of this. Yes, but in parties and events, this buzz seems to grow. It seems I am too popular.'

Aradhya let out a soft grin. 'Showbiz, ahaan. Interesting!'

Barkha laughed and nudged Aradhya's elbow, who murmured a soft 'ouch!'.

ꟹ

'Accha listen, Aradhya, do you know about the whereabouts of Anjali?'

'No. I thought you are in touch with her. I was for reasons, now known to you, not in touch with any of our college friends. First, Papa's postings, then the sudden marriage thing which had so many adjustments attached, and then Ravi's sudden demise... I have wandered a lot in these years.'

'No, even I haven't been in touch with Anjali all this while. All I remember is the time when she got married. The news came to me through a friend and I couldn't make it to her wedding due to some business assignments. Well, that's a long time back. It has been ages since I have seen or heard from her.'

'Hmm. Me too. We three were so close but due to so many different circumstances, we were left with no contact with one other. Luckily, I found you. Who would have ever thought of that? Small world!'

'Right. Anjali was the topper, yaar. She was a brilliant student, a scholar and the most creative of us all. I think she must have joined a reputed company or who knows if she's running a business of her own?'

'You mean to say she is a business tycoon now?' Aradhya asked.

'Haan! You can say that. After all, she was capable of achieving all that. She must be a bigshot now!' replied Barkha.

'Hmm... Well, to be true I tried searching her on Facebook and other social media platforms. But things went in vain. I couldn't trace her.'

'Even I tried contacting her once or twice, on her old number, long back. But they seem to be suspended now,'

Barkha admitted.

'Where can we find her now?'

'I guess we should try some other way now,' suggested Barkha. 'Old friends or college records might help us out. There must be some way to reach her.'

'I am sure she must be well settled in life now and independent too,' a puzzled Aradhya replied with a smile on her face. 'A big bungalow, expensive cars, a well-to-do husband…'

'Yeah! You are right. She was the best amongst us.'

'I wonder where she is now and I hope to bump into her soon, just the way we did!'

'I hope so too,' sighed Barkha.

7

Past Present Tense: Comparisons Make No Sense

It was an evening of leisure and celebration for the family. Arun, who was the second son-in-law in Aradhya's family, had been promoted and it called for a family outing that day. The entire family, including Aradhya and her two daughters, Arun along with his wife Anu and their son, the parents and Aradhya's younger brother Somesh, stuffed themselves in Aradhya's grey Innova. Luckily, they all fitted in. After that, Ram Singh was given further directions as to where to go. They had all decided to watch a movie at Inox and then have a sumptuous lunch at their favorite hangout, Barbeque Nation. It was all going well until the family, barring Arun decided to choose the topic of Ravi's memories to cheer up Aradhya.

'He was a good son-in-law. In fact, he was the best!' Aradhya's father exclaimed, just like on any other day. He would often sit for hours telling tales of Ravi's bravery, his near-perfect behaviour and the love that the family had for him.

'Not again!' Arun murmured.

'Did you say something?' Mr Sharma inquired.

'Oh no, Daddyji. I just agreed to what you said. Ravi was indeed the best!' Concealing the true feelings within his heart, Arun responded.

After all this is what he had been doing in all these years. It was not like that he didn't like Ravi or was jealous of him. In fact, he truly respected him. But the fact, that the family actually belittled him or his efforts every time they talked about Ravi was nowhere to be recognized by any of them. He felt sad whenever they said words like 'Ravi was the best. There can be no son-in-law better than him.' But since, this has been a norm and tradition for the family since years, he never ever could express his resentment. Even that day, which was actually *his* day, he chose to keep his mouth sealed and the family continued to blabber.

'Ravi was an ideal husband and Didi had been very lucky to have someone like him,' Anu said.

Sitting at a corner of a table, Arun silently wished the Ravi conversation would soon end. He felt miserable whenever his wife idealized Ravi. It seemed all the efforts that he made to keep his family happy were always unnoticed. No one seemed to bother about him or his feelings, and he continued to be a mute reciprocator to the entire family conversations.

'Yes, indeed!' It was now Somesh's turn to justify the statement, and in fact put a stamp of approval to what his sister Anu had just said. 'Not just an ideal husband and a good son-in-law, he was also the best brother-in-law anyone could ever have.'

Arun couldn't help but notice that Aradhya's eyes shone every time her family discussed about her late husband. Sometimes, he felt as if this whole Ravi thing was the family's best pastime. In fact, it never was clear to him whether the family did it deliberately, in order to bring a smile on Aradhya's face or was it just the other way round. Aradhya always seemed to cherish the moments. Her eyes did the talking every time these praises popped up and she seemed to light up with a sense of pride on being the wife of the *most ideal man* in this world. None of them were sensible enough to let go of the past.

This was actually not so unusual, if kept within the specified limits. There are many people who have become famous after their demise. People tend to start idealizing someone after they leave this mortal world. But this was not the case here, in this family. Since the very beginning to this date, even after years of Ravi's demise, they continued to idealize him each and every day, totally ignorant about Arun's feelings towards the entire thing.

Arun was upset thinking about the complete turn of events on his promotion day. He felt aloof and unimportant. Though the celebrations were in his name, but the centre of attraction was Ravi, just like on any other day. It seemed everyone in the entire family had taken a vow to belittle him every time they were together. His wife, Anu, was no exception to this rule. She kept on telling him how good a husband Ravi was and how lucky Aradhya was to have him. This outing in the name of a celebration party only added salt to his wounds.

∾

It was late in the evening when the parents decided to excuse themselves and go for a stroll. The ones left behind decided to order some booze and snacks.

'Well, congratulations, Arun. You did really well,' Aradhya said, extending her hand to greet her brother-in-law.

'Oh! They remember,' Arun thought and like a gentleman extended his hand, smiling to himself.

'We are proud of you.'

'Like Really!' He thought.

'What are you thinking?'

'Oh nothing! Thank you so much.'

Anu smiled.

'Seeing your family praise your husband is a good feeling. But does Anu really think so or is it just a sarcastic smile that she wears and still is comparing me to Ravi,' he wondered.

'Do you guys know something?' Somesh interrupted all of a sudden. 'Once Ravi helped me out with something in my hostel. He didn't even bother Mom and Dad with it. I still remember that day. Hats off to that guy, yaar!'

It seemed the happiness that had overpowered Arun all of a sudden was short-lived.

'Again? Here we go,' he thought to himself.

It was not the case of jealousy overpowering him. Neither did he dislike his family members for being a diehard fan of Ravi. In fact, he was the one who had once suggested Aradhya, years back to announce a new award in the Management Association in the name of Ravi, to which she had refused. As time fled, the family's attention towards the departed soul grew and Arun was all left to himself. He had started to feel aloof amidst it all. Not only forlorn, but he felt low whenever this Ravi episode cropped up. It seemed he had no place in their hearts. The only place that they ever had was reserved for Ravi. All his efforts to keep his wife and her family happy had gone in vain since Ravi's demise. He felt sorry for himself yet again.

This was not the only story behind his agony. He often felt that he loved Anu more than Ravi ever loved Aradhya. Okay, if not more, then not less also. But she never reciprocated his feelings in the same manner as Aradhya did. Her feelings for her husband had always been genuine and this reflected in her behaviour. Even till date, her face lit up whenever their family discussed about Ravi. This was probably the major reason for the traditional practice of bringing his topic and memories up to keep her happy.

Ravi was not the only reason behind their successful relationship. As per Arun, even Aradhya should have been given equal credit for it. She had always supported Ravi in every possible way. Whether it be physically or emotionally, she was never behind. But Anu was totally different from her sister. She never supported Arun the way she should have. In fact, she seemed to be praising Ravi for all his goodness in every gathering. All of this pestered him often, the result being a husband who closed himself in a shell at every gathering his wife was present.

Frustrated, he excused himself and took a seat somewhere at a distance. The family seemed to be happy without him also. It seemed his absence never made a difference to them.

'Hello, Arun,' a familiar voice disturbed his thoughts and he turned around to look.

'Pawan, long time, dude! How come you are here and

why didn't you tell me you are coming?' Arun seemed surprised and relaxed a bit, seeing his long-lost friend.

The duo were not only best friends in college, but were also amongst the brightest students. Pawan had shifted abroad for higher studies and Arun had managed to bag a decent job in Lucknow. The distance had put restrictions on the frequency of their conversations but still they had managed to share the important pieces of news relating to their lives with each other. Pawan was the only one who knew the story behind the frustrated Arun—the excessive adulation for Ravi and Anu's participation in everything that was happening.

'How are you?' he asked.

'I am all good, Pawan. How are you? Why didn't you tell me you were coming to India?'

'I just came back last night. Thought of giving you a call, but it was quite late. And then luckily, I saw you here. Hats off to the coincidence!' Pawan replied.

'Yeah, right! I couldn't have imagined this happening… at all! It's such a beautiful surprise.'

The two of them hugged each other and took their seats.

'So? Are you here with someone?' Pawan inquired.

Arun pointed to the other side of the massive hall. 'The family's here.'

'So why are you sitting alone here?' The fact that though Arun was accompanied by the entire family, still he chose to stay alone was alarming news for Pawan. 'All okay?' Any problem?'

'No, no problem. They are busy with their talks and I didn't feel like joining them,' Arun muttered in a voice that was barely audible.

'Arun, are you hiding something from me?'

'No. Why do you say that?'

'Because I know you very well. Tell me what's the matter?'

'Nothing, yaar! You know how these people are. Don't you? It's the same old conversation today. Nothing different. I feel so pissed off at times. I just cannot bear to hear the same thing again and again. Though I know this makes Aradhya happy, but still.'

'Hmm. So this is the case. Ravi. Right?'

'Yes. Right,' Arun answered softly.

'I understand how you feel. It must be really painful for you to be a part of such family conversations. I really empathize with you. These people should understand that all men are different. Everyone doesn't like PDA, some are silent caretakers too. It doesn't mean that they don't love their family. They very well value their relationships. It's just that they cannot display their emotions in front of everyone. But I guess, the world is full of exhibitionists. Even love has become a subject matter for display nowadays.'

'True. Sometimes, I feel they do not really recognize my efforts or love for the family. There's always that Ravi benchmark that I am compared to and I never seem to pass the test. Personally, I feel that the family is not allowing Aradhya to move on. They are just dragging her into the past every time they talk about Ravi.'

'You are right. Life cannot go on like this. Clinging to your past is never a good option.'

'But unfortunately, these people do not realize that. Actually these people are not even doing justice to Ravi.

According to Hindu norms, a departed soul should be allowed to rest in peace. Why do they remember him so much that a living person starts to feel insecure in their presence? I know even Ravi wouldn't have liked this, if he were alive. This is just making matters worse for me. Why put in so much effort into a relationship when no one is ready to appreciate or even notice it?'

'I understand your point. Actually, the modern woman needs a different kind of husband, someone who is also social. Someone with a ready smile, a firm handshake, a performing self.'

'Leave it, yaar. A famous economist J.M. Keynes once said, "In the long run, we are all dead." But I would like to modify it a bit here. "In the long run, we all are dead and good." In India, no one seems to care for what they have at present. Rather, they live in the past and cherish the memories. A living soul has less importance than a dead one. Same is the case here, in this family.'

'You are absolutely right, my friend. Distance does not ruin a relationship. Doubts do. Aradhya and her father are always on a single track... What a great man Ravi was! If Ravi was alive, what would he have done?'

Not just that, they even keep coaxing me to put all my property in Anu's name. God knows what they will do with so much property. Sometimes, I feel that everything is a money game. There are no strings attached.'

'Oh! I didn't know that. I am sure your efforts are no less than that of Ravi, when it comes to your family. I hope they see the truth, very soon.'

'No, I do not think so. They have made an admiration

society. Anyone who differs in opinion is labelled a bad man. Aradhya keeps on counselling Anu… Why do you listen so much to your husband?'

'Tell me one thing, Arun. Where are your parents? Do they know about any of this?'

'No, I don't want to bother them. They are in Lucknow.'

'What? Lucknow? You don't live with them?'

'No. Anu wanted to live near *her* family. I tried to explain it to her, but she was so adamant about it. I had to rent an apartment near them very soon. My parents live in our old house. I feel so guilty about everything. You know, these modern-day princesses, they never want to live with the in-laws. They never seem to be okay with the idea. It is said that girls leave their house after marriage but the truth, as I know it now is that they also make sure that you leave yours. Anyways, let's skip it for now. I am glad that we met. It feels so nice talking to someone so close.'

'True,' Pawan replied smilingly, placing a hand on Arun's shoulders.

The conversation lasted for a while. Pawan had a meeting in the late afternoon and he left with the promise to meet Arun. Arun felt a bit relaxed after the long and much-needed heart to heart and he went to join the others at the dining table. They seemed happy to have him back.

8

Ladies, Your Age Matters More Than You Think

The phone rang for a while before it awoke Aradhya. A casual glance at the bedside clock said it was ten in the morning. It was Sunday and Aradhya, like on every other weekend, was sleeping till late.

'Hello,' she answered the call, yawning.

'Hello, Aradhya.' It was Barkha at the other end of the receiver.

'Hello, Barkha. So early in the morning! Everything okay?' Aradhya enquired.

'No. I have some work in town today and I want to meet you after that. Will 1 o'clock be okay with you?'

'Argh, yes. Are you here for some official work?'

'Kind of. Let's catch up at Fun Republic Mall. I'll give you a call half an hour before I leave from here.'

'Perfect!' Aradhya said and hung on the receiver. 'What could it be?' she wondered.

ര

At around one in the afternoon, as was planned, Aradhya reached the destination and instructed Ram Singh to go back home.

'Mummy needs to go to satsang at around three in the evening and the kids have their extra classes at two in the afternoon. Remember the timings. I am going for some important work. I'll give you a call once I am done with it,' she said and Ram Singh nodded in approval.

Barkha was waiting for Aradhya outside the crowded McDonald's at Fun Republic Mall. It being a Sunday, the mall was a meeting point for couples. Amidst the crowd, the two ladies successfully managed to grab a seat as they ordered two aloo tikki burgers and a chilled coke with some fries.

'Haan, tell me now. You sounded panicky over the phone. Everything okay?' Aradhya enquired, taking a small bite of her burger and placing the rest on the food tray in front of her.

'Not exactly,' Barkha replied. She seemed crossed over something.

'What happened? Tell me in detail.'

'My boss. It's all about him.'

'Carry on. I am listening.'

'Earlier, it was only me he considered worthy of consulting before taking any official decision. And now, this girl... Priyanka. She has an edge over me. Everywhere...all I hear about is PRIYANKA.'

'And who exactly is this girl? Is she a newcomer?'

'Not exactly, but it's been a year since she joined our office. And since that day, she has been trying to woo Mr Kothari, my boss.'

'Is she beautiful?'

'No.'

'Then why are you jealous?' Aradhya smiled at Barkha, who seemed pissed off.

'Because she is young, smart and intelligent. She knows how to play her cards well and Mr Kothari is her puppet now. He never seems to find any flaw in her or any fault in her dealings. According to him, she is the best of the employees that we have had so far. What about me?'

'Oh! So this is the concern. Your boss is not paying any heed to your work or to you, to be precise. All the attention is drawn towards this girl, who is very young as compared to you. Both in her age and experience, right?'

'Correct. Not only that. She has been declared as the CEO of the company in our annual meet held a few days back.'

'What?' Barkha was shocked. 'Now, that is a major concern.'

'Oh yes! I feel little in front of that bitch. She has used all her means to get to that level and I know she won't be able to do justice to that role, ever.'

'Isn't Mr Kothari aware of your feelings? You have worked very hard to bring the company to this level.'

'That son of a bitch doesn't care for anything. All he needs is the fulfillment of his sexual desires. Even at this age, he gets plenty of action,' Barkha clenched her fist in anger as she uttered those words.

'So, do you mean even you have compromised?' Aradhya asked sipping from her glass.

'Everyone needs to. In the corporate sector, that is quite

common. You need to have a ladder to climb in order to taste success. Mr Kothari was one such ladder for me. But now, he has fallen for the charms of that young bitch.'

'Oh! So that's the complete story. Now I understand why you feel so dejected.'

'Shouldn't I?' Barkha raised a brow. She knew she wasn't wrong and she wanted the same kind of a response from Aradhya, who looked at her sympathetically.

'Of course, you should. After all, it was your position that she bagged. I can't imagine that asshole used you for so long.'

'Hmm. I don't know what to do now? Mr Kothari will not listen to me if I ask him to throw this girl out.'

'I agree. He is already in her trap.'

'I feel cheated.'

'I understand your situation, Barkha. And you are right in feeling that way. That monster has used you, fed on you and now, he has found solace in someone else's arms. This is absolutely not done. I think you need to teach him a lesson.'

Aradhya's words reminded Barkha of the time when she joined Fashionista. Since Day 1, she had tried her best to reach the top. She looked no less than a model and she frequently received compliments for her figure and complexion. Her slender frame, mesmerizing black eyes and shoulder-length hair lent her a quaint charm. To add to that, she was equally intelligent and had aged quite gracefully. It was a Monday morning when a senior had introduced her to Mr Kothari, her boss. Mr Kothari was a man in his mid-forties with smoky grey hair. Dressed in a designer suit teamed with a Rolex watch, he looked every bit a filthy rich guy. A pair of gold-framed round sunglasses hid his lustful eyes.

'Good morning, miss!' said Mr Kothari with gleaming eyes, taking off his glasses.

'Good morning, sir. Well, it's "Mrs" actually,' replied Barkha.

'Oh, you seem so young. I must say you have a wonderful figure. Well-maintained, huh!' he said, checking her out from top to bottom and almost undressing her with his eyes.

Her semi-transparent chiffon saree gave him a peep of her bare skin and she somehow liked the way his eyes hunted for more. Teasingly, she dropped her pallu to give him a quick preview of her heavy bosom and before he could recollect his senses, she swiftly adjusted it, apologizing in the most innocent manner ever.

'It's okay!' he replied, his eyes still stuck to her heaving bosom.

Barkha enjoyed the way his eyes feasted on her nude skin and the cool air in the room stiffened her nipples, the outlines of which were clearly visible under her pallu. Mr Kothari couldn't stop himself from staring at her tits. This was the first time Mr Kothari and Barkha met and it had triggered sexual desires in him.

She remembered her first business trip with Mr Kothari. She was supposed to deliver a presentation in front of some of the most important international delegates. Like usual, she wore a semi-transparent blue saree that day. To knock off the senses of the men seated in the presentation room, she had deliberately adjusted the pleats of her saree, a good couple of inches below the navel. The people present were watching the big screen attentively, until she distracted them with her deliberate sensual moves, drawing their attention to her exposed belly and navel. A tinge of excitement took over her as those men gaped at her. Needless to say, the presentation was a success.

It was not long after that when Mr Kothari called her to his chamber. She knocked at the door and he answered, breathing heavily, 'Come in.'

She entered the cabin and promptly shut the door behind her to avoid any sneak peek by the employees.

'Barkha, I was very happy with your presentation today,' said Mr Kothari, ogling at her breasts. 'But you need a little bit more training in that area. You see, more exposure for more success…' Mr Kothari replied with a big grin on his face.

'What kind of exposure?' Barkha questioned innocently, lowering her eyes.

'You'll get to know in no time. Come to me after the office hours and I'll teach you all.'

'I am ready to learn,' Barkha smiled and walked out.

In a matter of few days thereafter, she readily allowed herself to loosen up before him in return for financial and positional favours. It was not long before Mr Kothari had full access to the hooks of her bra and skin beneath the designer panties that she wore. One sexual favour granted to the old man meant one promotion for Barkha. This went on for long and everywhere, from office premises, to outdoor meetings, to even business trips abroad. Indeed, she was learning a lot!

Barkha had become the favourite pastime for Mr Kothari,

who would explore her deep sexy navel and round buttocks anywhere, anytime. A million times, the pervert had stroked her thighs and pulled up her dress to treat himself, and Barkha had no qualms about it as long as she got her share of promotions. It was very clear for her. The more the sexual favours, the more chances she had for a promotion. During those days, there was no one else to cater to Mr Kothari's lustful needs, other than her. It had been a secret that she had nurtured for long. Looking back, she now regretted those days when she had readily succumbed to Mr Kothari's lewd intentions, but she did benefit from that association as well. But recently with Priyanka in the scene, she had lost all her chances to woo back Mr Kothari, as he had willingly surrendered himself to the sparkly young talent.

All this flashed in front of her eyes and she struggled to wriggle out of her thoughts, in fact out of the situation that she was in.

'But how do I teach him a lesson?' she asked Aradhya.

'Do anything and get rid of that girl first. What's her name… Errh… Priyanka.'

'Mr Kothari won't let that happen.' Barkha let out a sigh.

'I guess you are smart enough to make it happen and I shouldn't be telling you this. By hook or by crook, you have to do this. Once she is out, you can once again have your own ways and yes, Mr Kothari will once again be yours,' Aradhya replied, her voice crisp.

'I think you are right. I need to get this girl away from Boss. Or else, she'll ruin everything I have had so far.'

∾

Till the time Priyanka joined the company, there was no looking back for Barkha and the whole office bowed to her orders, even Mr Kothari. But the situation was different now. Priyanka was the new face of Fashionista. She was bold and smart. Not that she was a divine beauty, only taller, darker and younger than Barkha, but she knew how to have her way and was brilliant at it. Not only that, she was also ready to compromise at any step needed to climb up the corporate ladder. Mr Kothari was merely a puppet in her hands and there was nothing Barkha could do about it. The girl who never had the word 'second best' in her dictionary had eventually become a second option for someone who had fed on her for years.

It was not that she cared for Mr Kothari, but yes, she did care for her career and craved success. This sudden turn of limelight from her to a young fresher made her feel forlorn and bamboozled.

Barkha's share of the burger was left untouched and she didn't even feel like having it. 'Enough of her,' she thought. 'I'll snatch back my position and power very soon.'

'Hello. Where are you lost?' Aradhya's words brought her back to the present.

'Nowhere.'

'Still thinking about her? Don't worry. I know you can do it and that pervert will soon know your worth. Priyanka is just a little thorn. It happens, dear. Thorns do hurt and you have to have them plucked before they leave a scar. I hope you get my point.'

'Argh. Very well.'

'So tell me now, are you feeling better?'

'Oh yes. I was so frustrated till this morning. That's when I called you up. I cannot tell anything about this to Aneesh. Even if I tell him half of the truth, he'll behave like a typical sant Mahatma and would advise me to accept the change.'

Aradhya smiled and gestured Barkha to have her share of the food. 'So you don't share anything with him?'

'Why would I? I know our views never match. We both are exactly the opposite. Opposites do attract, but they never come closer. So is the case with us. You know, Aradhya, sometimes I feel as if Aneesh has been cheating on me.'

'Oh! Really? And why do you feel so?'

'He has recently changed all the passwords to his social media accounts. Earlier, I used to get a sneak peek. But now I cannot log in into any of his personal accounts because of the password issue. I had done that a few months back. Not only that, I feel he keeps hiding things from me. From Gmail, to Facebook, to Twitter, and even the phone, everything is locked. Everything has changed between us. Why would he do such a thing if he was not cheating on me? I cannot believe it and I feel so broken.'

'That's really sad. I am sure he has some secrets and he is deliberately trying to keep you away from them.'

'You do feel so, na?'

'Yes, Barkha. I do and I feel sorry for you. You should directly ask him the reason behind all this. There's no point in keeping quiet. If you have a question, ask him. He owes you an explanation. There is nothing called a secret in a husband-wife relationship. It all has to be crystal clear.'

'Hmm. I even feel that Aneesh doesn't trust me anymore.

He doesn't even listen to me at times. I feel like shit when I say that I am losing my hold over him.'

'That's even more concerning, dear. You should not let that happen. It's the key to your happiness and you are letting it go so easily. That's not done!'

'I think I need to tighten my grip over him again. These days, he is having his way around, more often and this is not right for our relationship. He has a problem with everything I do and think. He never seems to understand me. Never do we have the same opinion. If I go left, he'll always be on his right. God knows why I married this man? I shouldn't have said yes to him, even if he were the last male left on this earth,' Barkha said, frustrated.

'You are brave enough to live with a man like him. I must salute your patience. If I were in your place, I would have divorced him. What is the point in living with a man who is so ignorant of your happiness? You are courageous enough to tolerate him. I am glad Ravi wasn't like him. He was just the perfect partner.'

'You are right. Anyways, I am glad we met. I feel relieved of the stress.'

'Hmm. Anytime, dear. Just give me a call and I'll be available. You can share things with me.'

'Yes. I know that. Accha, how is everyone at home?'

'All good. Arun, my sister's husband, got promoted yesterday at his workplace. We had a small get-together in the evening. It was fun being with the entire family.'

'At least you have someone to call your own.' Barkha sighed.

'Don't say that. You have your children besides Aneesh.'

'Yes. I do. But they have grown up now and need their own space. I am lucky they still listen to me. Anyways, I have my kitty ladies to turn to when I feel lonely. After office, we usually hang up together at my place or go clubbing. Life is fun. It has always been, till this drama queen arrived in our office.'

'Leave her now, Barkha. Don't waste your time on such trivial matters. It's only a girl. I know you can handle things well. Stop thinking too much about it. After all Mr Kothari should be taught a lesson and he needs to know his limits.'

Barkha forced a smile. She remembered all the moments she and Mr Kothari had spent together, discussing the microscopic details and decisions relating to the company. Not a single leaf dared to budge in the office without her permission. And only she knew how much she had worked for it. 'How could he do such a thing to me?' she wondered. 'What will the entire office think of me now? Of course, I cannot allow Priyanka to take over all that I had once possessed.' The tag of being 'the best' was what she couldn't afford to part with.

'Hello, Mrs Lost. You seem to be lost somewhere, yet again,' Aradhya snapped her fingers, bringing Barkha back to the reality. 'What did I just say? Did you hear any of it?'

Barkha smiled. 'What? I know, Aradhya, I need to act very soon. Thanks for charging me up. That Kothari, he took me out for vacations so many times in the name of business dealings when I knew he just wanted to check me out. Business was secondary for him. It was I who made the company prosper. My decisions, my rules, my management. He was such a brainless creature always. And now, he has proved the same and I need to show him his true position. This position belongs to me and to no other roadside girl. What does she even know about the company, its policies and Mr Kothari?'

'Now that's like a geared-up woman. You should always fight for your rights. No one can use you like this and leave you feeling dejected.'

'Correct. And everyone should know that I am the real boss, and not Mr Kothari. He is a mere puppet who has worked under my name and suggestions all these years. He doesn't even know the B of business. The internal policies even, all were designed by me. He only knows how to monitor them and keep a check on their implementation. That featherhead has made a big mistake choosing Priyanka over me. She can never replace me. Never ever, in her entire life.'

'I know, sweetie. There can't be another you. After that award you got, Mr Kothari should have known better. His hard luck, he didn't.'

'Hmm. You just wait and watch, Aradhya. I'll get back my position and power in no time. Probably, even before the annual meet. I'll make sure I do that,' Barkha smirked and the two let out a hearty laugh.

9

The Cute Old Couple Syndrome

As the morning rays caressed his cheeks, Arun opened his eyes and found that his phone had been ringing since long. He stretched his hands to grab his phone, which was lying at one corner of his bed. One glance at it, and he knew it was Raunaq who had been calling him for quite some time. There were three missed calls from him. Raunaq Ahuja was Arun's ex-colleague from his old company and also a dear friend. He had recently become a novelist and his book *Just Don't Do It* received both compliments and criticism. Arun answered the call in a voice that sounded sluggish.

'Hello, Mr Arun. Where are you? I have called you thrice before this.'

'Hi, Raunaq. Sorry, yaar. I was sleeping.'

'At this hour? It's ten already!'

Arun glanced at his watch and knew Raunaq was right. He hasn't ever been this sleepy before. 'Actually it was quite late when I went to bed. Some pending office work. You know how it is. Right?'

'Oh yes! What about our meeting today? I am coming

over to your place at one in the afternoon. Will you be there? Don't say no. It's been long time since we met and besides, it's a holiday today,' Raunaq insisted.

'Why not! I'll be more than happy to see you. Yes, it's been quite a while. Are you coming alone or with Bhabhiji?'

'No. I am neither coming alone nor with Amrita. A friend of mine is coming along. She is an independent journalist and her name is Rubina.'

'Oh ok. You're welcome. I'll wait for you.'

'Ok. Bye. See you.'

'Bye,' Arun ended the call. He flung his bed sheet to one side and looked around. Anu was nowhere to be seen. Instead, he found a note stuck onto one of the doors. It read: 'I am going to meet Aradhyadi. Will be back by evening.' Arun read the piece and threw it in the bin kept at the corner of the room. He was happy he wasn't invited to join a Ravi-centered conversation this time. At least, he could have some time for himself while Anu was away.

൴

At around 1.30 p.m., the door bell rung. It was Raunaq along with a girl about his age. She wore a casual black-and-red striped shirt, teamed with blue denims over a pair of black flats. Behind the frameless specs that she wore, Arun could see that she was hazel eyes. The colour of her hair was in perfect sync with the colour of her eyes and she looked extremely inquisitive. 'After all she is a journalist!' Arun thought and smiled to himself.

'Hello, Mr Author. You are late.' He hugged Raunaq and shook hands with Rubina.

'I am extremely sorry. We were stuck with some mediapersons,' Raunaq replied.

'Oh no. I can understand. You are a big name now. Fan following, huh?' Arun teased his friend and gestured his guests to sit down as he himself took a seat next to them.

'Nothing of that sort, dear,' Raunaq replied calmly. 'It seems to glisten, but it's not like that. To be true, there are more critics than admirers.'

Rubina nodded in approval. 'He is right!'

'I have read the book, Raunaq. It's very well written. And moreover, it displays the true scenario that we have today. Why would anyone criticize it?'

Raunaq's book was based on the relationships between men and women in the present era. Needless to say, it was a topic of debate for many. There were many who liked it because of its harsh but heartfelt confessions, yet there were a lot who criticized it for being male-centric. Rubina was the one, who although being a woman, had truly liked it! She had approached the author with reviews and they were friends since then.

'There are plenty of reasons, Arun. Not only that, but many have been telling me it is only my frustration being revealed through this book.'

'What? Seriously?' Arun asked with a tint of dismay. 'I wonder why people have such a narrow view of things. There is nothing wrong in what you wrote.'

'Hmm. Even I think so too,' Rubina said. 'This is such a different concept and outlook. The book has all the qualities that can do wonders. I wonder why people get into creating so much nuisance.'

Arun nodded his head in approval. 'Anyway, tell me, Raunaq, how was this book-writing experience?' he enquired.

Rubina too looked at him with gleaming eyes, whilst he turned away his gaze coyly.

'Writing was the last thing I had expected to do. But there were a few aspects of society that I thought could be better expressed if written. And men-women relationship was one such topic that captured my mind since very long. It's not my frustration, but my feelings and thoughts that I have expressed and I have no regrets for penning it down,' Raunaq replied. 'Yes, there's a lot that I can say about the publishing industry here. It's full of people who are ready to deceive you, at every step. Arun, I had faced so many difficulties with the publishing of the book.'

'As in?' Arun seemed more interested all of a sudden. He sat upright as Raunaq spoke.

'Arun, there are many publishers who lure you into buying attractive packages that they have. They charge a hefty amount from you and once you are done with the payments, they have nothing to do with you or your book.'

'Gosh! Do you mean everyone is like that? Even the big publishers that we've heard of?'

'I ain't saying that, Arun. But yes, the big publishers have a reputation. Why do you think they would want to publish the work of a debutant author like me?'

'You are right. They often seem to be busy with publishing books of renowned authors.'

'Correct. Moreover, these days, we have so many celebrities coming up in this field. Some of them have actor-husbands. They earn in crores and it's a cakewalk for them to market their books. Do you really think we can stand amidst them? The marketing expenses these agencies charge is quite hefty for us, if not for them.'

'There seems to be so much of this. I never thought it could be that difficult,' replied Arun.

'It's not very difficult but yes, you need to be extra cautious while dealing with people.'

'And what about the book reviews?' Arun questioned, looking puzzled.

'Well, the people have started to respond to it. But I am afraid there are many who are not taking it well. I have mails from admirers as well as critics. Some loved the flow of words and to some, it seemed more like a portrayal of resentment.' Raunaq turned to Rubina, who showed her approval to what he was saying with a blink.

'I personally liked the book a lot. And I have told this to Raunaq a number of times,' she added. 'Nothing personal. Yes, but there are a few questions in my mind that I would like to clarify.'

'I could even relate to Arjuna, the main character in the book. His characterization was so natural. Now look at me, Raunaq. You know the facts, dear. The truth about my relationship with my wife is not hidden from you. And we've discussed it earlier, many a time. Right?' Arun turned to Raunaq for an answer.

'Right. I know how Anu is. You have told me earlier. Is she still the same?'

'Unfortunately, yes. In fact, differences between us have multiplied over the years,' Arun said with a look of remorse in his eyes. Suddenly his phone rang. 'Excuse me, guys,' saying this, he went out to take the call while Raunaq and Rubina continued with their conversation.

'What's this with Anu, Raunaq? Is there some problem between them?' she enquired.

'Argh, yes. Sort of,' he replied. 'Tell me, Rubina, why do women want to get married?'

'Umm. I guess, it's because of the want of love.'

'To some extent, you are right. Women need love and care throughout their life and there is nothing wrong in it. But they are so obsessed with marriage. Do you know why? It's because they require a man to take care of them, always. A woman knows that she needs to acquire someone before her charm vanishes. A man, however, can attract any woman till the time he is earning good and has equally good resources. For a woman, this window is comparatively small. It's only till the time she is pretty or attractive. After that, no one would want to look at her. Now, how do they ensure that they have that man who would take care of her for the rest of her life? The answer is marriage. It's a very simple thing. For women, marriage is the ultimate female social orgasm.'

Rubina was quiet when Arun returned to the hall. 'Sorry, guys, to have kept you waiting.'

'Doesn't matter. Who was it?' Raunaq enquired.

'Mr V.K. Singh. Remember?' Arun said, looking into his eyes.

'That Mangina!' Raunaq exclaimed.

'Yes. He was asking me if we could meet and I told him you are here. I agreed to meet him. I hope you both are okay with it. Sorry, I replied on your behalf.'

'Oh, no, no. Don't be sorry. It's been a long time since

I met him. Let's call him over,' Raunaq said.

'He is coming over to Golf Club and has called us there. I guess, it will take us about half an hour from here to reach there. What say? Chalein?'

'Chalo! We have all the time today...' Raunaq replied and looked at Rubina, who nodded in approval.

'Chalo! But wait a second. I didn't get you guys. What's that word that you just said? Mangina?' Rubina interfered, sounding confused. She had never heard that word before.

'You'll get to know when you meet him,' Raunaq smirked. 'Let's go now!'

ೋ

Mr V.K. Singh was a man of average height, about the age of 40. He always had a number of girlfriends throughout his life. He was the kind of a guy who could talk all nonsense to please a woman. Or to put it correct, he could say whatever it takes to impress a lady. He was a man with a pronounced feminine side and that's why the word 'Mangina'! Raunaq told Rubina all about him as they drove to Golf Club.

'Hello, Singh sa'ab. How are you?' Raunaq hugged him as soon as they met at the entrance gate.

'Hello, Raunaqji. You are a big shot now. *Kabhi hume bhi yaad kar liya kijiye.* Do remember us also at times,' Mr Singh replied, shaking hands with Arun and Rubina.

'She is my friend. Rubina. She is an independent journalist.' Raunaq introduced Rubina to Mr Singh and all of them exchanged quick smiles.

'So, Raunaqji. How is your book doing?' Mr Singh asked.

'Bas, enjoying the best compliments and criticism that

one can think of!' Raunaq smiled.

'I have heard a lot about it,' admitted Mr Singh.

'Well, thank you! I take that as a compliment.'

'So, Arun, how is life?' Mr Singh now turned to Arun, who sat at one corner of the table with a glass of sweet lemonade.

'*Bas pacha rahe hain, Singh sa'ab. Farq sirf itna hai ki kehne ko meetha hai.*' Sensing what he meant to say, everyone let out a hearty laugh.

To Rubina, it seemed that the traumatic phase of Arun's life was known to all his colleagues and friends. Even Mr Singh seemed familiar with the husband–wife relationship that Arun and Anu shared, and she too, knew a part of it now. Suddenly, her gaze turned towards an elderly couple right across their table. The husband was helping his wife take a seat. 'How cute! This is what is called as companionship. I guess it's the thing that you need the most as you grow old,' she exclaimed and the other three turned to have a look at the scene that fascinated her so much.

'How cute!' Arun mimicked Rubina. 'These women, they don't stand by you when you need them at the prime age, but they have fascination for an elderly couple that they see. Where do you think this is coming from? Well, I will give you the answer. This is nothing but their insecurity that crops up with age.'

Rubina was taken aback by this sudden remark from Arun. She looked at Raunaq for help.

'Do you know, Rubina, why girls love such emotional scenes so much?' Raunaq asked.

'I guess it's because they are very sensitive beings. You can explain to me the other opinion also, in case you have any.'

'What I believe is,' Raunaq continued, 'that men and women reach their prime at different ages.'

'Kindly explain,' said Rubina and the other two also looked interested in what he had to say in response.

'Women are at their prime between the ages of 20 and 40. At this age, they tend to control men with the most powerful weapons that they have, that is beauty, body and ultimately, sex. The appetite for sex in men is at its peak at this age. However, they tend to become wise in their forties. You know what they say...naughty at 40. Well, it's because at this age, they become more mature and have a different perspective on things around them. After being used by women, who bribe them with sex to fulfill their desires, they learn to control the flow of blood, along with their testosterone. It should be brainy and resourceful at 40! Because successful men are in the prime of their career and can control resources at this age.'

'What about women?' Rubina enquired. 'Don't they become mature with age?'

'Oh yes! They do. But with the increase in their age, they start losing their charm too. They know that they cannot control men any more and hence, the only bond that can be present is that of emotional support and companionship. Rubina, men don't look for sex in relationships after 40. They search for emotional hook-ups. The source can be any. Even a tawaif, a prostitute, can provide an emotional support that men crave for. They really do not care about the source of this support. Sex, ultimately becomes secondary. It can be a part of the support system but definitely not a stand-alone.'

Rubina listened quietly all the while Raunaq spoke.

'You know, Rubina, the institution of marriage has been laid down mainly for the benefit of women in society. The main reason being to provide companionship to them after their prime age. But unfortunately, the other sex doesn't seem to realize this. The result is that gradually with time, men are more likely to opt out of this system called marriage. Even the court has sanctioned the legality of the live-in relationships now.'

The young journalist was all ears but she definitely did not agree with the entire observation, but yes to some extent, it did seem correct. Rubina had never given a thought to this side of the story. She wondered if what Raunaq said was true.

'Women love to play the victim. Take any example. Be it the Rohtak sisters or the famous Gurmehar Kaur controversy. I hope you have heard about those…'

Rubina nodded in approval. Her thoughts flashed back to the entire controversial videos that went viral years ago.

'But I think, Raunaqji, that it is the way we perceive things,' Mr Singh interfered, trying to be friendly with the beautiful lady sitting next to him. 'Earlier, the freedom of choice was only with men. Now, the whole scenario has changed. Even women can choose the person with whom they want to share things, work with or even bed,' he said, looking at Rubina, and she smiled back.

She agreed. 'It's not a male-dominated society anymore. Even women, today, are rejecting men for various reasons. They have their own choices and I think it's completely okay.'

'These things happened earlier too. Only the difference being that it was either the upper or the lower classes of society that were affected by it. Now, the things are permeating the middle class too,' Raunaq replied. 'Men are supposed to be providers. Why don't women marry the delivery boys or the helpers and live with them? It is because they want trophy husbands. Everything should be served on a platter. They don't prefer raw materials to work with. According to them, an eligible man is one who has sufficient resources to cater to her needs as well as those of her children. No girl generally falls for a guy who is not well off. Even rich ladies prefer to be seen with more resourceful men, even though they can marry a poor guy. A person serving tea in a restaurant is not the one that they would usually prefer. Men are always judged by their wallet and how fat it is, their height and family background, whether in love or arranged marriage.'

Rubina wanted to interfere but an important call suddenly diverted her attention and she excused herself to take it.

Meanwhile, Mr Singh gulped down the last of the many vodka shots that he had ordered and turned to Arun. He said tipsily, 'I keep on telling Raunaq not to take this call of something being right or wrong. One should just enjoy life.' The strong smell of alcohol could be smelt of him as he spoke. 'I don't know why, why on earth does he waste his charms over a small matter like this.' Mr Singh said, pointing a finger at Raunaq. He held Arun tightly and murmured, 'Arun sa'ab, I can bet, I can bet that Raunaqji can woo any girl, any girl with his suave looks. You understand na. *Koi bhi ladki*. But he always seems to be more interested in changing everyone he meets,' saying this, he slumped onto the floor.

Arun looked at him, gobsmacked whilst Mr Singh continued. 'Arun sa'aaab, no one ever changes in this world,

I am telling you. Make no mistake... You know, American style, huh!' he said, demonstrating the whole thing with the movement of his hands. 'So what's the point explaining? Which woman in this world wants to hear that she is wrong? Tell me. So use them and I bet they will love you back.' He blew a flying kiss to Raunaq, who kept his lips sealed all the while to avoid any explosion. 'Raunaqji, if you can please a woman by abusing a man, why not do it? I say, DO IT. Thoda sa feminism hi to chahiye to sleep...sleep with them. *Romani hune ke liye aaj kal feminist hona jarrori hai,*' he murmured, highly inebriated. His eyes had a strange sunken look and he fumbled with his words as he spoke.

Both Arun and Raunaq looked at each other, perplexed. There was no way to stop Mr Singh from spilling the truth and he continued in a hushed voice. 'Sshhhh...' he said, closing his eyes and gesturing the others to listen. 'Let me share an incident with you. Yesterday, a girl was abusing Raunaqji for his book. I haven't read the book, yet I supported her adding four more abuses and she hugged me in no time. "The world needs men like you and not that moron Raunaq." That's what she told me,' said Mr Singh, smiling to himself. 'Thanks, Raunaqji for this favour, my shop will run till there are men like you and females are fools. I know that you are a good guy who wants to help people, but who cares for good people like you,' he spoke, looking intently at Raunaq.

Nobody!

'Waiter...*Do...do peg aur meri taraf se.* Two more shots on me,' Mr Singh called out, holding onto his empty glass.

10

Different Rules for Singles and Doubles

'Why don't you say something?' Raunaq nudged Arun, who was still looking at Mr Singh, dumbstruck.

'I guess enough has been said already.'

'Sorry, guys, to have kept you waiting,' Rubina smiled as she approached the two, tucking a strand of hair away from her face. 'So, what did you talk about and what has happened to him all of a sudden?' she asked pointing to Mr Singh, who seemed highly inebriated.

Mr Singh smiled back nervously.

'Leave him, Rubina. He's a bit drunk,' said Raunaq.

'A bit?' she asked, confused.

'Accha, tell me, Arun,' said Raunaq, trying to deflect Rubina's attention, who still was looking at Mr Singh with disgust. 'What do you think about the married women thing that I just said? Do you agree with it? Do you think on the same lines...that women fail to provide emotional support to their husbands?'

'Not at all, I presume. What I think is that it's the

single independent women who are polluting the minds of the married ones. Please don't take it otherwise, Rubina,' Arun replied.

Rubina didn't like the statement that Arun just made. She was hurt and couldn't resist questioning his remark with a raised brow. 'As in?' she asked.

'I just feel that both the categories of women, the single and independent ones on one hand and the married ones on the other, have their own set of experiences, and there is absolutely no comparison between them. The married women take suggestions from the single girls out there, who make suggestions according to their own perspective, which is strictly not done. There are different problems and different coping mechanisms for both. Women need to understand and respect this fact to avoid any sort of misunderstanding. The suggestions from the alpha females often lead the beta ones into a troubled marriage. You can take the example of Aradhya, Anu's sister. She transformed herself from being a beta to an alpha female after her husband's demise. Whatever the reason, let's not get into that. But now, when she should ask her sister to support her husband, she is encouraging her ways instead. It seems she has forgotten herself in the past few years.'

Rubina looked at Arun, who blurted out about his feelings and to be honest, they were rather harsh for a girl to digest.

'I once read a work by Paul Elam,' he added. 'According to him, women say that everything is about patriarchy. But it's a theory still seeking validation. And it will never find it's place. Patriarchy is all about gynocentrism. Patriarchy is women and children first. And even the same thing is coming out of female ideologues now. Men need to step up. They need to support women. They need to do this. They need to do that. Where do you think this ideology is coming from? It's the same thing as patriarchy, coming out as a different idea. It's like meet the new boss, the new boss is same as the old boss! All this has been stated by Paul and I totally agree to it. Yes, indeed patriarchy is about gynocentrism. Old wine in a new bottle. I hope you are getting what I am trying to convey.'

'And where is that thought about single woman coming from, Arun?' Rubina enquired. 'What you said about patriarchy, even if I agree with it, what do you have to say about the independent woman? Why do they occupy such a low position in your outlook?'

'No, Rubina. They don't occupy a low position. In fact, I don't even have a problem with their independence. But you see, they are polluting the minds of the married ones, who in turn ruin their happy families.'

'And how is that?' she questioned.

'The married ladies, they tend to take the single, independent women as their role models, instead of taking the successful homemakers as an example. That's the prime reason why such ladies were segregated from the society. Nowadays, it's not like that. And that's why I say that single girls often are found to be polluting the minds of the married ones.'

'So, do you mean all the single girls or ladies out here are to be blamed?'

'No. I am not saying that. It's just that women are not

mature enough to compare the lives of the two. The life of a single lady is totally different from that of a married one. There is actually no comparison. The truth is that the independent ones are not able to come out of the age-old patriarchal thinking and the married ones use them as a shoulder to cry upon.'

'And what do you think of the single guys? Are they also the same?'

'Single men do not go about demonizing women and polluting the minds of married men,' Arun replied. 'I agree, some single men may be spoilt. They go to brothels, bars and discos, have relationships with call girls. But then, they don't create rifts in the lives of married people. But women, if they are single, they want to see every other woman on this planet single.'

'Oh! Do you really think so? I have never thought of it,' Rubina replied.

'Yes. I can explain. Aradhya was a perfect wife all throughout her married life. But since Ravi's demise, there has been a complete change in her. Anu looks up to her sister in awe and takes her as an example to follow.'

'So, do you mean to say that being independent is wrong?'

'No. All I am trying to say is that married women should know and understand the difference between their lives and that of single women. They should also learn from women who are perfect homemakers. That…that is, taking care of one's family…according to me, is the most respectable job in society.'

'Do you realize, Arun, that independent girls also leave

everything behind, even their parents, to adjust in a new family? It's cruelty to separate a married man from his parents, but it is a tradition to separate a girl from everything, even her own family, after marriage. Is that justified?'

'Yes. I agree that women have to leave everything behind when they get married. But they also try and mould you so that you leave your family. Just look at my wife. She did just that. She coaxed me into leaving my parents in order to live with hers. What would you say to that? I have been suffering so much because of that family, which lives in the past, rather than in the present.'

Rubina was quiet for a while. Arun was not wrong either. It's true that there were instances like this happening everywhere and these were actually ruining the image of women in society.

'Is it the same with them even now?' Raunaq enquired, worried. The conversation had grown intense and he didn't want to interfere all this while.

'Well, my wife thinks that I don't love her, not as much as Ravi loved Aradhya. But she fails to understand a simple thing...that in order to be loved by a husband in the same manner, the wife also has to be someone like Aradhya. Now, she has turned into a narcissist. To Anu, I was a villain the moment I refused to live next door to my in-laws. Imagine, my parents are living alone in our old house. I don't think Ravi would have ever preferred that, if he were alive. Visiting the in-laws once a while is okay. But living with them is altogether a different thing,' Arun replied morosely.

'Arun sa'ab...' Mr Singh interfered suddenly. 'I only know that two things are vital in a relationship...respect and compassion. The problem with single women is that they are narcissists and are also egocentric in nature. *Inko lagta hai*, they feel that they are doing something out of this world by living alone and being independent. They are constantly looking for compliments from people around them.'

'Is that why you have so many girlfriends, Singh sa'ab?' Raunaq questioned naughtily with a wink. 'Because you compliment them well?'

'Raunaq ji,' replied Mr Singh, fumbling with his words. '*Aaj aapko ek raaz ki baat batate hain.* The secret of V.K. Singh. *Ek kitab soch raha hu likh hi du.* I am thinking of writing a book. Social media sites are the best places to find such partners. You just have to spot the right girls—girls who post regular selfies, beaming with pride and confidence, like air hostesses. *Samajh jana yahaan demand hai.* Then it is simple. Just flood them with compliments.'

'And she'll be your friend?' Raunaq questioned, rather unbelievingly.

'Nahi, Raunaqji. It's a highly skilled job. First, you have to identify such narcissists, then slowly give them the bait, try to figure out what's missing in their lives and slowly provide them with the needful. Along with tons of compliments, don't forget! There is only one caveat. Don't try to mould them to your will. Just nod at whatever nonsense they say, praise them for their courage and beauty, and seduce them...'

'But, I...I only tell them the truth because of my love and concern for them,' Raunaq protested.

The other three looked at Mr Singh in disbelief.

'*Raunaqji, gyaan ki baatien koi nahi sunta hain aajkal.* No one likes to be preached. Just tell the girls what they want to hear and use them. It's actually quite simple,' Mr Singh smirked.

'What rubbish is he talking about?' scoffed Rubina, clenching her fists and struggling to control her temper.

'People often say the truth when drunk, Rubina. Let's not get into that. Leave him alone,' Raunaq suggested. He turned to Arun and said, 'So, tell me, Arun. What were you saying?'

'Raunaq, I have a very clear opinion in this matter,' replied Arun meekly. 'I have some expectations from my wife. I have been adhering to all her wishes since long. But she needs to understand that every human being is unique. In fact, every husband differs from the other. They all have different temperaments. I cannot please everybody all the time. Ravi was an extrovert and I am an introvert. But that doesn't mean I don't love my family. I love my family, just as much as he did. And just being different doesn't make me a demon.' There was an intense look in his eyes as he spoke.

'The family needs to realize that I am a human and not a saint. They cannot keep on hurting my feelings by regular comparisons with Ravi. Sometimes, I feel like putting an end to my life. It's Ravi who deserves to be with them, not me. They are so stuck to the past that they really don't care about their present or the future. They have no consideration for the living soul sitting right next to them. You know, I tried many a time to please everyone by doing what Ravi used to. But my efforts went in vain. And now I think that I need not put so much effort into my relationships when there is not even a single word of appreciation for me. Whatever I do, the comparisons are bound to resurface, as always.'

The others could sense disappointment in Arun's voice as he spoke.

'Here, I wish to say something,' Mr Singh added meekly.

'Not again,' murmured Rubina, holding Raunaq's hands.

'Rubina madam. I speak no wrong. There are very few things that a man looks for in a short-term relationship with a woman. The breasts, the butt, the personality. All we need is an attractive body. But when it comes to long-term commitment, we have higher standards and expectations. The women who constantly dress up like a cheap tart are mostly kept in the former category. Girls in miniskirts, low-cut blouses and heavy make-up, and with raunchy behaviour are all included in that slot. These are all responses to a man's short-term list. And to be true, even I adore such girls. But to attract a man for a longer term, a woman should have an idea of his long term preferences. I have had many girlfriends in my past, and I know the difference between them and my wife. The expectations are different, I tell you.'

'So true, Singh sa'ab. This is what the long- and the short-term expectations are all about. And, Rubina, the truth is in the initial years of marriage, when a man is physically involved with a woman, he is usually driven by her beautiful features, as Singh Sa'ab just mentioned. He is blind to her imperfections. If he's wining and dining with her or courting her, he's usually so high on dopamine and other hormones that everything else ceases to matter,' said Raunaq. 'But again, this "pussification" varies in degrees depending on the maturity of the man. As they become more and more mature, they tend to grow out of these shackles and the only thing that matters to them is emotional support from their partner. Women, on the other hand, as they age, develop a liking for younger men. Take for example Savita bhabhi. I hope you all have heard of that character. But what they fail to understand is that the attraction towards these young boys is purely physical and that is because they are sex starved. If Ravi were alive, he too would also have been "pussified".'

'*Aap to bahut gyaani hai,* Raunaqji. You are so intelligent,' smiled Mr Singh. 'I want to touch your feet. *Kahaan hai aapke paire?*' Mr Singh was finding it difficult to control his movements and he slumped onto the floor with a thud.

'He is totally drunk. I guess we should leave now,' said Rubina as she stood up to leave. 'You need to drop me back, Raunaq. It's quite late.'

'Please take care of Mr Singh, Arun,' said Raunaq.

"Yes, I will, Raunaq. Bye now.'

11

Big Boys Don't Cry: Really?

An infuriated Barkha was sitting cross-legged on the sofa with her hands on her head. She had complained of a severe headache and had asked Aneesh to stop irritating her.

'I have said what I felt, Aneesh, and you need not give me instructions. I am fed up of your interference in the way I bring up my kids.'

'Barkha, I am not interfering. But please understand. I beg you not to teach Ayaan the lesson of male shame.' Aneesh replied. There was practically nothing he could do about Barkha's parenting style, as she always turned a deaf ear to any of his suggestions. But still, it was a different day and a different matter altogether.

The conflict related to their son Ayaan. In a trivial fight between Ayaan and his sister, the latter had lost her cool and hurt the former with her words. Feeling the agony of being insulted by his sister, Ayaan had complained to Barkha, shedding a drop of tear or two. He was hurt, but his mother didn't care. All she noticed was tears rolling down her son's cheeks. '*Ladke hoke rote ho?* Being a boy you are crying?'

she had said. What she said disturbed Aneesh, who was having his breakfast alone, as usual.

'He is hurt, Barkha. And what's wrong if he chose another way to express his emotion? He didn't hurt Nivedita back, right?'

'Look at you, Aneesh,' Barkha sounded as cold as ice. 'You are saying this? I can't believe it. You are also a man and you know very well that no one approves of a man crying. It's such a shame for boys to deal with things like this. *Ladka hoke rota hai*. Being a boy he is crying. What will people say? I don't understand what your problem is, Aneesh. Why are you teaching him things that will ultimately make him lose his dignity in society?'

'I am not teaching him anything like that, Barkha. I am just trying to say that he is still a child. In fact, a developing mind. Why are you instilling wrong notions in him? *Ladke rote nahi hai*. Boys don't cry. What is all this you are teaching him? By saying something like that, you are actually teaching that men are not supposed to show their emotions. Not just that, you are telling him that even if he is really perturbed by something in life, there'll be no one to help him out with his emotions.'

'Look,' said Barkha, annoyed. 'I am only telling him what society teaches us. And by crying like this, he'll not only bring shame to himself but will also drag us into humiliation. I don't want that, Aneesh. These are the basics that a boy should know and learn. And I approve of it. It's about the society that we live in.'

'But who created these rules...that a boy is not supposed to cry? Whenever a thing like this happens, I always find the parents dragging their boys and telling them that *ladke rote nahi hai.* Where is this all coming from?'

'Shut up, Aneesh. Enough of your philosophizing. I have had enough of your lectures. Please do not piss me off any more. I am in no mood for an argument. It was a trivial matter that you turned into a big issue,' Barkha scoffed.

So precisely the idea of male shame was always shrugged off by Barkha and the matter was unwontedly shut. The phone bell rang to finally announce the closure of the same.

Barkha picked up the receiver and a familiar voice at the other end greeted her. 'Hello, Barkha. I hope I am not disturbing you.'

'Oh! Hi, Aradhya. No, not at all. Please tell me,' Barkha replied, sounding as calm as she could.

'Nothing so important, dear. It was Sunday and I thought you might be free for a chit-chat.'

'Yes. Absolutely. Anyways, it's been a long time since we met,' said Barkha, gesturing Ayaan to go and wipe his tears. He left without creating a fuss and Aneesh was left feeling helpless.

'Yes. It's been long and I was missing you since morning. By the way, how are Aneesh and the kids?'

'The kids are doing good and Aneesh, as usual, interfering too much,' Barkha said, making deliberate eye contact with Aneesh, who stood just a few inches away from her.

'Don't worry! Things will soon fall in place,' Aradhya assured her.

'Oh! No, Aradhya. I am not worrying. I know how to tackle my problems. Anyways, how are your kids? I must say you have brought up your daughters like sons. A big salute to you.'

'Argh! Thank you. It was tough though.'

'And I must also admit that your daughters are in no way less than boys, Aradhya.'

'Thank you so much, dear. I feel happy when someone says that. It feels like my parenting has been successful. You see, I have always raised them up like that,' Aradhya replied, feeling rather proud of herself.

'Hmm. I can see that you have geared them up for the future. I am very proud of you, Aradhya.'

'*Accha, chod ye sab.* Forget all that, Barkha. Tell me, how was your day?'

'Oh! I have a terrible headache, yaar. I had a fight with Aneesh right before you called.'

'Why? Is everything okay?'

'Not exactly. I am fed up of Aneesh interfering in anything and everything that I do. He keeps finding faults in me all the time. I just scolded Ayaan because he was crying over a petty fight he had with Nivedita. Now, you tell me, Aradhya, does it look nice? I mean a boy is crying. People tend to laugh at things like this. What will they think of Ayaan? He is a grown-up now and needs to learn how to control his emotions.'

'Right. Boys are not supposed to be cry babies. If he'll not learn at this age, people will mock at him later. You did the right thing, Barkha. I have never seen a boy complaining and crying like that. What did Aneesh say? Don't tell me he said you were wrong.'

'Oh yes. He did say that. He thinks I am inculcating in Ayaan a feeling of male shame. Can you believe it? And even if that's what I am teaching him, our society approves of it. He is going to be a part of this society after all and he should know these things.'

'Hmm...I agree with you,' Aradhya uttered softly.

'I am disheartened that Aneesh turned out to be such a bad father,' Barkha replied with a sigh. 'I expected him to be a bit more sensible. He is so impractical. And I really don't want my children to grow up to be like him.'

Little did Barkha know that Aneesh was standing right behind her, all this while, listening to the entire conversation. He felt disheartened and hurt, annoyed and insulted, all at the same time. He wanted to pour his heart out, but Barkha's words 'Boys cannot express their emotions like this' kept ringing in his ears and he sat down on the chair with a thud.

Events from the past flashed in his mind—events from the time he married Barkha. He had expected a happy life with her. And in all the years of their marital life, what he had received from her was great humiliation. The tag of him being an immature and insensible guy was deliberately pasted on his forehead by his dear wife. His heart sank as he remembered the number of times he was humiliated by her in front of their own children. There was no respect for him in his own house. He was made out to be someone who scolded his children unnecessarily and who brought out the worst in them. Whatever he said, the children never cared to listen. Be it about studies, or sports, or general preaching on life. They were under the full control of their mother. Everyone noticed that he was an angry bird, but no one really bothered to find out the real reason behind his anger and frustration.

'And what was it that Barkha had said about raising a daughter like a son?' he pondered.

Aneesh may have failed in his role as a husband and a father, but he surely was a man of principle. From the whole conversation that his wife had with her friend, he concluded that girls were constantly being compared to boys, when according to him such comparison means degrading a gender. Whilst you quote the famous dialogue from *Dangal—Mhari choriyaan, choron se kam hai ke?*' you unknowingly tell your daughters that they are an inferior gender. 'Why does society have such expectations from girls?' he wondered. Barkha was mother to a daughter and a son, yet she made such comparisons between the two genders. Why should anyone create a rift between the genders by saying 'My daughter will now play the role of a son'?

Aneesh wondered if there were teachers like Barkha in schools. 'How will the children turn out to be then?' he thought to himself. He couldn't imagine the single feminist teachers being the guiding force in the development of children in such schools. The feminists who themselves have escaped the merits of a family system, he wondered how they would teach a child the basic essentials of a man–woman relationship in the long run. For the first time, he felt thankful that Barkha was in the corporate sector, but again he shuddered at the thought of a single independent 'female' teacher being the guiding force behind a child's value learning system.

The scene of a girl crying in a restaurant flashed through his memory. Years before, he had been to a restaurant. He found a girl crying. People had gathered around her, trying to console her. Aneesh wondered what the scenario would have been like if it was a guy crying, not a girl. People would have mocked him for sure. But why? Probably because, men have been shamed over and over again. He thought. Their pain is invisible or as a matter of fact it is tabooed in our country. At a very tender age, the basic principle of male shame that 'big boys don't cry' is instilled in them. They get this idea that their feelings are not something that everybody would like to hear about. When a girl says she wants a man who is touched by his feelings, what she actually means is that she needs a guy who is touched by her feelings and helps her out to deal with things. The agony of Barkha's words had left its imprints on his heart and Aneesh left the house without dropping a word to his wife about it. She was still busy with the call, unaware of his presence or absence.

ꕥ

'What are you saying, Aradhya? You have got Anjali's contact? How in the world did you manage to find it?' Barkha exclaimed over the phone. She was still busy talking to her friend over the phone.

'Yes. It was through a friend of Arun that I got hold of her contact number. Raunaq Ahuja. He is a novelist. And all this happened just by chance when one day I bumped into him at Arun and Anu's anniversary party,' Aradhya replied joyfully.

'So does he know her?'

'They are friends. And I happened to know this when I saw her picture in Arun's photo gallery as he was flipping through his old photographs. I asked him and he admitted being friends with her. The last time we met, we were discussing about her and look, I have finally found her contact. This is called luck by chance!'

'That's great news. Have you called her yet?'

'No. Not yet. But yes, I surely will. And I wish we meet her soon. The third friend in our college group. Oh! It's really been ages since we three met. I am already excited.'

'Yes. You are right. Even I can't wait for that reunion. I wonder what she is doing at this moment.'

'Me too,' Aradhya murmured. 'I bet she's into something grand.'

12

Empowered Offices: Ruined Homes

'I want to meet this author. Umm, what was his name? Raunak Ahuja?' said a young lady to her colleague. The lady was in her mid-thirties. She adjusted her black-rimmed glasses and kept the book that she was reading on the table.

'Well, in that case, Anjali, there's some good news for you,' the colleague replied promptly.

'What?'

'He is from Lucknow and I can get you his contact.'

'And how will you do that, my dear Elena?' Anjali enquired, raising a brow.

'Contacts, sweetheart! Don't worry. I'll get back to you with his number. Just give me two minutes,' saying that Elena left with a mischievous smile. She dialled a number while Anjali waited impatiently for her to return.

After few minutes, Elena handed Anjali a piece of paper with something scribbled on it. 'Here it is!'

'Whoa! That was quick.'

'See, I told you!' Elena chuckeld. 'You need to have contacts to get your work done. By the way, why do you want to meet him?'

'Because, my deal girl, he is an author who has written something I don't approve of.'

'As in?'

'He is an anti-feminist, Elena, and according to me, he has written a lot of bullshit about women in his book. I want to meet him and discuss certain things with him. He needs to know what a waste of money and effort this book has been. He is a good writer and could have written about a better topic than this crap... Oh! Someone's calling me...' said Anjali, excusing herself to take the call.

Anjali Mathur was a confident lady working as a vice president with a reputed company in Lucknow. She was the mother of two and her husband adored her. From position to power and status, she had everything. But there was something missing in her life. Though she never tried to find out what it was, she knew there was something missing.

'Hello,' said Anjali as she picked up the receiver.

'Hello, Anju. We are waiting for you outside your office. We had a plan to dine out tonight, remember? It's already 8. Where are you?' It was Akhil, her husband.

Anjali had completely forgotten about her plans with her family. She was stuck the whole day with some important presentation and now, at the end of the day, she was too tired for anything.

'Akhil, I am very tired to go anywhere now. You please go ahead with the kids. I have already called the driver to take me back.'

'Anjali, that's not fair. We had made the plan to sort out our differences, to spend some quality time with the kids.

Even I had an important meeting lined up, but I managed to spare time for you, for us. The kids will be disheartened to hear that you are not coming.'

'The children are more sensible than you, Akhil, and it was you who made this plan, not me. Don't you understand I am too tired for anything? Don't make a fuss in front of the kids and please leave. I'll get some gift on my way for the kids to make up for all this.'

Akhil banged his fist on the steering wheel of the car. This was not the first time he had had to deal with such last-minute developments. Anjali's negligence towards the family had always been a major issue, often leading to conflict between the couple. She had always been excessively career oriented and unfortunately, the family had to suffer a lot because of that. Apart from her job, everything else had always been secondary for his dear wife, whether it was him or their family. Her relationships had no importance in her life. And this day was no different. The only connection that the children had with their mother was a materialistic one, but Anjali failed to realize that.

Akhil left for dinner with his children, as was planned, and Anjali headed home. She was fast asleep by the time the family returned. The kids collected their gifts from outside and Akhil, just like on any other day, slept in the drawing room.

The next morning, Akhil woke up a little late. The maid was busy doing the household chores. '*Mem sa'ab chali gai, sahib.* (Madam has left for work),' she said, handing him his morning cup of tea.

'*Haan, pata hai. Tum apna kaam karo.* (Yes, I know. You continue with your work),' he said, feeling frustrated.

Every morning, he felt that the maid deliberately reminded him of the fact that his life was incomplete. Her words had started to pinch him now. He felt miserable, reminiscing about the past. He was extremely happy the day he got married. But his happiness was short-lived. Anjali had soon begun to show her true colours. Not that she was a bad person, but she was a very ambitious and career-oriented. Too much for any regular family to handle. Not only that, she always tried to emerge victorious every time a conflict came up between the two of them. Akhil gave in to her fancies without protest, because he wanted a happy home for his family. But Anjali mistook it for his helplessness and cowardliness. She pestered him with words that pinched his heart. Either she was busy with her work or she was simply too dominating for him to feel at ease. Either way, he did not have many memorable moments with his wife. Even the birth of their daughters didn't bring any change in his wife's attitude. She was still the same. She still couldn't take out time for her family. The children were growing up to the whims and fancies of the maid and Akhil was helpless about it all. In the initial years, he had taken regular leaves from his office to look after the kids. But, unfortunately, this was not possible in the long run and ultimately, it was the family who had to suffer because of Anjali's indifference towards it.

Akhil recalled his sad past as he steadily drove towards his office.

~

'So, did you call Raunaq?' Elena asked Anjali during recess.

It was time for the employees to relax but Anjali was,

as usual, busy fiddling with her laptop.

'I am talking to you, Anju.'

'What?' Anjali asked, without bothering to turn around.

'Did you talk to Raunaq?' Elena repeated her question.

'Who Raunaq?'

'Look at you! Till yesterday, you were trying to get his number and now you don't seem to remember him even. Raunaq Ahuja, the author. *Kuch yaad aaya?* Do you remember now?'

Finally, Anjali took a break from her work and turned to look at Elena. 'Oh! That anti-feminist person. Yes, how can I forget him? I do have to meet him once to tell him what I feel about him and his book.'

'And what do you feel?'

'I feel it's a total crap. I told you, right?' Anjali was blunt. 'He has written so much about women, but all in a wrong way. The choice of his words shows that he is a frustrated guy. Someone who is highly disappointed in his life, someone who has no other motive than to downgrade the position of women in society. I think I really need to meet this guy and teach him a few things.'

'Have you talked to him yet?'

'No, not yet. I was too tired yesterday. So much so that I slept like a log the whole night.'

'And what about your dinner plans with Akhil and the kids?' Elena enquired.

'To be honest, I was so preoccupied the whole day that I forgot all about it till the time Akhil called me up. But then, I was too tired to join them.'

'Oh! So he must be upset about it, right?'

'I don't know. When I left home this morning, he was still asleep. So I couldn't have a word with him. But I brought gifts for the kids on my way back yesterday. I hope they liked it. Anyway, Elena, these things don't bother me much. Specially, Akhil. He is a grown-up. He can take care of himself. I am already pissed off with my work and life. The conflicts that we have only add to my misery. It's better if we stay away as much as possible. In that case, there will be no room for arguments. And I think Akhil doesn't understand me at all. We are two different identities with different sets of ideologies. Whatever I do, he seems to find flaws in it. So, what's the point spending time with someone who doesn't even understand your ambitions and dreams?'

'Hmm. Right. You are a working woman. He should at least respect that. You can't do everything for your family.'

'Unfortunately, he doesn't respect that, Elena. He is a self-centered man with old-age ideologies. I am a modern woman and I like to live life on my own terms. I have my own life and why should I sacrifice it for anyone else? But Akhil is every bit a family man. He believes in ancient traditions, joint families and all that stuff, which are beyond my imagination.'

'How did you fall for this guy, Anju? You both are so different.'

'Ours was an arranged marriage. I had protested, but my pleas went in vain. I had to tie the knot before Papa's retirement. So that's the reason why I fell into all this. But it's time to build my career now. Family is not the thing that I can afford to focus on now. I have my own dreams to fulfill. But these regular conflicts between Akhil and me are driving me nuts, I tell you. There seems to be no solution to our problems. It is not that I don't want to be with my husband, but it's just that the differences are too much to handle. A ruined relationship with my husband is what I have now and I want to stay out of it.'

'I bet you'll be at peace if you leave him,' Elena smirked.

'I can't say about it but yes, I am on the lookout for someone.'

'Accha, the recess is going to end very soon. It's already 2 p.m. How about a cup of coffee?'

'Hmm. I guess that would be perfect before I carry on with my presentation,' Anjali replied, allowing a faint smile to form on her lips.

'Do let me know if you happen to meet Raunaq,' said Elena with a grin.

'Of course, I will. By the way you didn't tell me. How in the world did you get his number?'

'Arey no secrets, yaar! He is a close friend of my friend.'

'And who is that friend?'

'Arun. By the way, it's my birthday next week. I am going to invite Arun and I would like you to come over as well. I can invite Raunaq even, if you say. That way, you'll get a chance to meet him also. It would be a change for you too, only if you are okay with it.'

'Oh! I would love to,' Anjali replied, enjoying the last sip of her coffee.

'Great! Chalo accha, now let's get back to work. I'll let you know the plans very soon!'

'Sure,' Anjali replied and promptly headed back towards her desk.

13

I Am Sorry > I Love You

It was a packed room. Most of the people were unknown to both Raunaq and Rubina. Though they were invited to this event, they had no clue about anyone present there, except for Arun.

'Why in the world did we agree to come here? Rubina said with dismay. 'I am feeling so left out.'

'Be calm, Rubina. We are here with Arun and that too because of a humble invitation from Elena. There must be some strings attached. And just look at Arun, he seems so happy being alone,' Raunaq smirked, pointing at Arun, who was busy conversing with the handful of people that he knew.

'Hello! How are you, Raunaq?' A voice like melted butter brought them out of their boredom. 'I am Elena. And I asked Arun to bring you guys along to this party.'

'Do you know me?' Raunaq enquired.

'Yes, of course! Who doesn't know you? Your book is doing really well.'

'Argh! So whose side are you on, miss? The admirers or the critics?'

Elena smiled. 'None, actually. To be honest, I haven't read the book till now.'

Her instantaneous yet unanticipated reply surprised Raunaq a bit. 'Then? How do you know me?'

'My friend, Anjali,' Elena replied, pointing to a woman in her mid-thirties. Anjali waved at them from a distance and excused herself from the crowd to join them. 'She has read the book and wanted to meet you personally. I am sorry I didn't have your number, so I asked Arun to invite you on my behalf.'

'No issue. By the way, happy birthday,' wished Raunaq, extending his hand.

'Thank you and thanks for coming,' replied Elena.

'I have wanted to meet you for a very long time, Raunaq,' said Anjali, who had by then joined the trio in their conversation. 'I have read the book, to the last word. You may not like what I say next, but I was really appalled by what you wrote.' Trying to be careful with her words she said, 'You seem to be a nice guy. Then why all this crap?'

Raunaq could catch a glimpse of disgust in her eyes as she uttered those words. 'So, you are on the critic's side. Well! There are many like you and I wish I could meet them too,' Raunaq sighed.

'Yes. How can you expect an anti-feminist work like yours to be appreciated by anyone?' Anjali scoffed.

'Let me put it rightly for you, dear,' Raunaq replied. 'I am not anti-feminist, dear, and neither do I dislike women. If you really have read the book and understood it in its true sense, which I am sorry to say you haven't, you would have known the depth behind my choice of words.'

'Do you call it "choice"? Well, I call it sheer hatred towards a group,' she replied, her voice curt.

'That's how you interpret things, Anjali. It may be anti-feminist shit for you, but to me, it is more about love and equality.'

'Well in that case, dear, I would like to argue with you further on this topic. I want to make you realize that the piece you wrote and call a book, is just your hard feelings towards women in society and nothing else,' Anjali said, giving Raunaq a cold look.

'Sure, I would love to answer your questions,' he replied and the three of them steadily made their way towards an isolated area amidst the group of people who seemed to be packed like sardines in a can. Rubina, who followed the two, gestured Arun to come over and he followed suit with a drink in hand.

'So, Mr Raunaq, tell me now. What were you saying?' asked Anjali.

'You were saying something about my book, dear. Tell me. I am eager to hear your opinion.'

'Well, what I was trying to say is that you are a chauvinist, Raunaq, and I don't blame you for that. Men tend to be like this, barring a few. Whatever you have portrayed in your book, I don't agree to it. The fact is that the relationship between men and women has always been unequal and oppressive with the former having an upper hand in it. It's just that the extent of inequality and oppressiveness varies. Have you not seen men who are dictatorial?' Anjali raised the question.

'Tell me, Anjali, has your father or brother or husband ever oppressed you?' asked Raunaq.

'Never. In fact, my mother was an alpha female and so am I. But that doesn't mean that things do not revolve around men. Men tend to dominate the other sex.'

'What is patriarchy all about, dear?'

'A system in which the male dominates the female.'

'Do you realize that women are themselves asking the men to step up? They need to protect their daughters, mothers, wives, and are even considered to be responsible for their entire welfare. Where do you think this ideology is coming from? Patriarchy is women first. In your words, if men are responsible for the betterment and security of the other sex, how come you say it's about male domination? Don't you think it is more of gynocentrism than male dominance? And if you have never been oppressed by any male in your life, why do you say that the females have been oppressed. You yourself admitted that you are an alpha female. Am I right?'

Anjali listened quietly while Raunaq continued. 'Despite the fact that 90 per cent of the divorces are initiated by women for various reasons, men are still required to pay her alimony, even if he did not want to destroy the union in the first place. Defenders of the system of alimony insist that a woman seeking divorce should not see a drop in her living standard after the divorce, but it is somehow acceptable if the husband sees a drop in his finances, even if he did not want divorce. Do you still call it oppression?'

'I am a working woman, Mr Author and all major institutions have been characterized by male dominance. Take anything as an example...the economy, any political system, family or religion, anything. They all have men as the ruling power. Don't you think this is an example of male dominance in society?'

'Here, I would like to ask you something. Do you get less salary as compared to your male counterparts? From your attire, you seem to be quite comfortable financially.'

'That's because I toil hard for it. In fact, many of my contemporaries are junior to me. I got promoted fast.'

'That is exactly what I am trying to convey. Just look at Vidya Balan. She takes home almost ₹5.5 crore for an ad. Do you still think that society is characterized by male dominance? Don't get swayed by Western ideologies. Women have been conditioned to such an extent that they have started to believe that all the ideologies support only male dominance. Tell me something, Anjali. Has your husband ever tried to dominate you?'

'I am an alpha female. Why will he dominate me?'

'Anjali, I am not saying that men don't commit crimes. Yes they do, but then they are criminals and should be hanged. Not the entire male population should be cursed because of a handful. Such beliefs only make women disrespect men, wives to think poorly of their husbands and girls to devalue the importance of their fathers and brothers. Why spoil your life for things that have not even happened to you? Why do you think women expect chivalry from men? During the earlier times, providing emotional support to leaders and army officers who fought for the nation was a huge task. I guess, that is why the thing called chivalry was there. Dear, respect is a quality that is expressed both by the person who demonstrates chivalry and those who receive it. But I am really sorry to say that there are many anti-male statements being made today, irrespective of the fact that in reality most men instinctively treat women with chivalry and out them on a pedestal. There is more chivalry than misogyny exhibited by the male population. Can't you see that?'

Anjali pondered for a while. Raunaq did talk sense.

'Tell me frankly, when was the last time you spoke to your husband? Have you ever given a thought to what he expects out of this relationship?'

Not knowing what to say next, Anjali preferred to stay quiet. It had been a long time since she and Akhil had a real conversation. There were frequent misunderstandings between the two of them, but she never gave much thought to finding its solution. Even Arun and Rubina chose to stay quiet that day.

'I am not anti-feminist, Anjali, and I say this again. I believe in equality between the genders. Tell me, dear, what do you think about love in a relationship?'

'It is important,' Anjali replied calmly.

'Yes, it is. I don't say that people think love is unimportant. As a matter of fact, they are starved of it. There are several romantic movies and love songs that we watch in awe. But I am surprised that there is hardly anything that we crave to learn from them.'

'What do you mean by that?'

'What I mean to say is that most of the people see the problem of love primarily as that of being loved, rather than that of loving. The expectation to be loved exceeds far beyond the capacity to love back. In fact, being lovable today is being a mixture of being popular and having sex appeal. People think that to love is simple, but to find the right object of affection is quite a back breaker. Am I making sense to you?'

'Yes. Carry on. I am listening.'

'In the modern world, the definition of love has changed quite a lot. The new concept of freedom in love has greatly enhanced the importance of the object as against the importance of function. Let me explain it better. When two strangers fall in love, the feeling is considered to be the most exhilarating experience in life. And needless to say, this type of sudden intimacy is often accompanied by sexual attraction, which unfortunately doesn't last long. And eventually, disappointment and boredom kill the relationship.'

'And what do you think is required to master the art of loving?'

'It's easy. You have first got to realize that loving is an art similar to music and painting. To learn how to love, you must proceed in the same manner like you do while learning an art. Love, you got to understand all about staying in rather than moving out. In a relationship, people refuse to give without expecting favours in return. What I believe is that "equality" today means sameness, rather than oneness. Both have different meanings.'

'You seem to know a lot about love, Raunaq!' exclaimed Rubina, with a twinkle in her eyes.

'It's all about life, dear,' Raunaq whispered with a smile.

'But life is not all about love. There are few who even destroy the basic element of respect in a relationship, no matter how much you love them. What do you have to say about it, Raunaq?' Arun enquired.

'Are you talking about Anu?' he asked.

'You could say that...' came the reply.

'Look, Arun,' interrupted Rubina in an accusatory tone. 'I didn't interrupt you the last time we met, because it was our first time meeting and I barely knew you. You were grief stricken and I allowed you to pour your heart out. But there's something I need to tell you.'

'What is it?' Arun asked, puzzled.

'Men like you are solely responsible for your condition. And I am sorry when I say this.'

'No, you need not be. But please explain. How am I responsible for what my wife is doing?' Arun sounded perplexed by the sudden accusation Rubina charged him with.

'Do you know what actually the problem is with you guys?' she said in an infuriated tone. 'The real problem is that men are so pussified that they don't empathize with fellow men. During their entire life, they are running after girls who use them. Men are rewarded for believing that their willingness to sacrifice everything, in order to gain a woman's approval, actually proves the worth of their manhood. For you, finding the secret to make a woman happy is eventually much more important than recognizing the fact whether your wives are good as a partner or not.'

Arun nodded in approval.

'Do you realize that the most important words in a man–woman relationship are not "I love you" but "I am sorry. I regretfully say that we Indians are so obsessed with Bollywood that we tend to follow all the shit that is shown in these movies. I remember the movie *Maine Pyaar Kiya* from our era. No sorry and no thank you is what Salman had said in retort to Bhagyashree's nasal, childlike response to a gift he had given her. Well, it sounds pretty romantic. Isn't it? But if you ask me, it is sheer nonsense. Tell me, how in the world are you supposed to make your partner, whether man or woman, accountable for their deeds?'

'But, Rubina,' Arun interrupted. 'I tried my best to…'

'No, Arun. You yourself are to be blamed for your condition. You could have firmly asked your wife to live with your parents, asserting that that's the only way for her to live with you. Or you could have simply asked her sister to stay out of your family matters. Aradhya chose to be an alpha female because she had to survive, but the same theory doesn't apply to Anu. Your wife has a husband who is very much alive to take care of her and the family. Her changeover from a beta to an alpha female is simply not justifiable. It is you who let her loose and then you cry over spilled milk,' said Rubina affirmatively.

'So do you mean to say that I should have taken charge of this whole thing? Am I really to be blamed?'

'Yes, you are, Arun,' replied Raunaq. 'There are many men who I have seen reacting emotionally to everything in life. They do not know how to take responsibility for their actions, if their life is dependent on it. Lack of accountability in any relationship is very common these days, but let me tell you one thing. When you are in a committed relationship, accountability is the only proof that you care about the feelings of your partner. Whereas, lack of accountability is a proof that whatever claim one makes of caring and loving a person is questionable. What Rubina said is right. Even I believe that the most important words in any relationship are not "I love you" or "I forgive you", but they are "I am sorry".'

'Very true. I agree with Raunaq,' Rubina asserted in a gruff tone. 'I am a girl, but I say that a demonstrative lack of accountability is a message that your partner will repeat whatever they did to you. If Anu has nothing to apologize, she practically has no reason not to do it again. And you ought to realize this, Arun. It's high time you comprehended these things.'

'I get what you are trying to say, Rubina. I have made a fool of myself all these years and I accept this fact openly. Only I am to blame for it,' said Arun, feeling rather low.

'Arun, self-respect in any relationship is important. You are in a relationship to be happy, to smile, to laugh and to make good memories. Not to be constantly upset, or to feel hurt or to cry. And this is what you have been doing so far. Very few men make this unsolicited disclosure that they were credited with lack of accountability in their lives. Unless questioned, they generally would not speak about it. There is a connection between Anu's lack of accountability and you being okay with everything that went wrong in your relationship. Every individual should take responsibility for his or her actions. Even your wife needs to understand that she needs to owe the entire responsibility of her shit in order to get back things to normal. There are so many who lack the skill to do anything for a happy relation.'

'So what should I do?'

'Just talk to your in-laws and Anu', asserted Rubina. 'Sometimes you have to speak up instead of suffering silently. As far as I can understand, everyone in your wife's family is trying to please Aradhya, even at the cost of your happiness. I am not an expert in relationships but two sisters living next door with their families is not a good idea. It is better to leave some space for relationships to grow, otherwise there is unwanted comparisons and meddling in day-to-day affairs, which ruins the relationship. If Aradhya is telling Anu, "Why do you listen to your husband?" "Ravi was the greatest husband ever!" Anu is being brainwashed into not loving you. Anu is also to blame. Why is she letting someone interfere in your relationship? Anyway, sorry if I have said something to hurt you, but truth is truth. The rest is your call.'

'No, don't be sorry. I am, in fact, grateful to you. I can see where things have gone wrong. I feel I am also to be blamed. The frustration of being compared was so much that it manifested in my irritable and bad behaviour. I am glad we discussed this. Had it not been for you and Rubina, I would have probably ended my life,' Arun said.

'Arun, do watch your behaviour, as it also reflects in your professional domain. You should pity Aradhya and her parents that they are living in the past. You must understand that in order to make Ravi great, they will belittle Lord Rama also. So take charge of your life,' Raunaq asserted.

Anjali, who was quiet all this while pondered over the reality of her married life. She hasn't been able to enjoy marital bliss in all these years. 'Was it my fault?' she thought. The evening and the entire conversation had left its imprint on her mind and she decided to give her relationship a second chance and try to work things out with Akhil. 'Excuse me, guys. I need to go now. It's quite late. It was a pleasure meeting you all. My family must be waiting for me,' she said as she got up to leave. 'And, Raunaq, we'll catch up some other time. Probably very soon!'

14

Men Are Talking: Are We Listening?

It was late in the evening when Anjali returned home after the party. 'Have I been so insensitive all these years?' she thought. A casual glance at the watch told it was 9 p.m. There was still an hour left for Akhil to return home. She decided to prepare palak paneer for him, his favourite. It was long since Anjali had left cooking. When she got a hefty paying job, she hired a maid, Shaanta, to do all the household chores, including the cooking. Though the family never quite liked the cooking, they had no other option. She had been adamant to change her decision and that's how Shaanta took charge of the whole house, including the cooking part. But this day was different. For the first time, she felt her cold feelings thaw as she wanted it to be different.

'Shaanta has for the first time cooked something really well,' said Akhil as the family sat together for dinner after what felt like a coon's age.

'Shaanta is on leave today. I cooked,' Anjali replied meekly.

'Who? You?' Pretending as if he heard something wrong,

Akhil asked, taking a pause from his bite.

'Yes.'

'But why? Didn't you have any important presentation to work on today?'

'I am thinking of resigning, Akhil.'

Akhil, who was busy helping himself to another serving of the palak paneer, put his plate down and looked at his wife in awe. 'Are you okay, Anjali?'

'Yes. I am.'

'So, what do you plan to do now? Are you joining another organization?' he asked again, not believing his ears.

'Umm…you can say that. Looking after the family is what I am planning to do now, and forever, and ever.' Her words came as a bolt from the blue and Akhil couldn't help but stare at her in disbelief.

'Are you serious, Anjali?'

'Yes, Akhil. I know what I am saying. Don't look at me like that. I am already feeling guilty for my negligent behaviour in the past.'

Akhil, who still felt it was all too good to be true, held her hands gently. 'Why do you say such a thing, Anjali? What's the reason behind this self-realization all of a sudden?'

'It's just that I feel we are not able to give time to the kids, especially me. In the course of running after the job and increments, my responsibilities towards you and the kids have been left far behind. I want to fulfill them now, Akhil. I have understood what I have missed in all these years and I feel sorry for myself,' replied Anjali, cupping her face with her hands.

'Well, if that is the reason, I am glad that you have

realized it before messing it all up. Family is the most important thing in this world, Anjali, and you need to realize its worth.'

Anjali kept quiet. For the first time, she wanted to listen to the other side of the story. She watched Akhil in admiration as he continued to speak. 'My dear wife, let me tell you something. The culture in which you have lived so far, is designed to make you fail as a wife. Alpha females aren't new. The world may need them, but I don't. In your case, you have always been an alpha prototype which means masculine and masculine energy tries to conquer whereas the feminine energy which is the beta type nurtures and verbalizes. And this is a universal fact that the masculine energy acts and the feminine responds. No man wants a boss or competitor at home. A relationship where both the partners are "alphas" comes crashing down in the long run and this is a fact. Do you know why? It's because in order for a man to own masculinity, you'll have to stick to your feminity. It isn't that attire doesn't matter. In fact, the more feminine you'll look, the more attractive you will be to your husband. There will always be conflict if the lady is an alpha, which means the dominating one in any relationship. Anjali, work is about money and marriage is about love. If you wish to make your relationship work, you need to take off your "I am incharge" hat and surrender to love at home. When you do this, you'll automatically find peace everywhere.'

'I feel apologetic when I look back, Akhil. There are so many moments that I have missed. With you, with the kids, with the entire family. Just because I have been working on important projects, I missed out the most important things in my life. I have always felt that you do not respect me or my work, but I was wrong. You did all you can, to keep me happy, to make our relationship survive. Whereas, the only thing that I craved for in life was power, and I feel repentant when I say so,' said Anjali in dismay. Her deep eyes reflected how much she felt sorry for the past.

'Do you know, Anjali, a man, whether he is a CEO or a handyman, wants to make his wife happy more than anything else in this world? It's what he lives for. As a matter of fact, a good man wants his wife to be happy and satisfied more than anything else in this world. He can go to any extent to make it happen. Not only that, he will also support his wife's ideas, plans and opinions, and that's because a man's number one goal is to please his wife. If he finds that his wife is impossible to please, then, I tell you, that marriage is in trouble. And let me add, you being an alpha means that you are impossible to please and this makes me feel like a jerk. If we talk about marital conflicts, you'll know that the prime reason behind such disagreements is the power struggle between couples. Two people wish to drive the same car, which unfortunately doesn't work. So, ultimately the only way to put an end to the struggle is for one partner to sit in the passenger seat. And mind you, by that I don't mean the back seat. Do you get the difference?'

Anjali nodded.

'You know, dear, marriage is a contract by convention, either by the respective families or by a marriage broker. Love is supposed to develop once the wedding has concluded. The assumption that there is nothing to be learned about love lies in the confusion between the initial experience of "falling in love" and the permanent state of "being in love" or you can say "standing in love". You can also say that love is an activity. It is "standing in" and not "falling for" love. There is fine line between the two. Anjali, understand that there's a natural synergy in a marriage when the man is more dominant than the woman. If both try to dominate, love and companionship in a marriage will be a distant dream. And this has exactly been the problem in our marriage.'

'Then why didn't we discuss this earlier, Akhil? Was I too difficult to persuade?'

'Unfortunately, yes. In fact, all the alpha females are. The betas, as compared to the former, are more patient and easy-going. They are easy to handle and are more laid-back. Sadly, Indian culture no longer gives importance to the beta females. However, I believe that they are happier and comparatively more relaxed and easier to get along with than the alphas. Because of their special characteristics, they don't struggle much in their relationship with their partners…'

'But I was doing all this for us. For the family,' Anjali protested.

'Why, dear? When I am there to take care of all our needs, you actually don't have to bother about anything in life. Your family should be your priority. It is a responsibility to be cherished, not to be taken for granted.'

'But that is why we have hired Shaanta. To take care of the house and look after the family in my absence,' replied Anjali, who was finding it difficult to hold back her tears.

'It is not Shaanta's duty to take care of the family, Anjali. The family needs your attention and love, sweetheart. It is your duty that you have belittled so far, running after your ambitions and power. See, this has been a problem. By nature, you are a maximizer, which is part and parcel of being an alpha female. You tend to step out in search of better choices and options, whereas the best thing you could do as a wife and mother is to be satisfied with what you already have.'

As Akhil spoke, Anjali kept staring at him, her lips sealed. It was all new to her. For the first time, his words, suggestions and reactions made sense to her, because this time, she actually wanted to listen to him. 'Why didn't you say something earlier, Akhil?'

'Because you are never in a mood to listen. I even tried sharing about my office life with you. But you took me to be a negative thinker. Well, I am not the kind of person you think me to be. I just want to share my feelings with you. That's it. But just because I don't express my emotions the way you do doesn't mean that I lack the ability to feel. In fact, men are deep. They just don't express their emotions or crib. It is as simple as that. A woman must understand this side to a man, if she wants to find peace and contentment in her relationship.'

'Hmm. I do get what you are saying. It is understanding between a couple that can actually elevate or degrade their relationship.'

'True. And let me tell you something else. Men crave for respect and women for love. If either of the two fails to deliver the desired, a relationship will not sustain. Respect that a man yearns for throughout his life is unfortunately not given by alpha females, which leads to conflicts. Anjali, men are much simpler to understand than a woman. What they want most is respect, companionship and sex. If you can provide a man with these basic needs, they'll go to any extent to keep you happy. In the absence of these, problems tend to arise. In fact, it is a crazy cycle. Without respect, he reacts and without love, she reacts. You tell me, Anjali, when was the last time we created a good memory? Or when did we actually talk?'

'I don't remember. I was always too busy to realize all this.'

'I felt neglected all the while you were busy with your office stuff. And then when you came back home, you were too tired to reciprocate to my feelings. Yes, Shaanta managed the household chores well in your absence, but we needed you, not her. A maid cannot substitute my wife or the mother of our kids. We said nothing, because you were too preoccupied with your work. But that doesn't mean we didn't feel neglected.'

'I am really sorry for everything. I never meant things to be this way.'

'You don't need to say that. But, there are things that you need to understand. And understanding and accepting the difference between the genders is one of them. Otherwise, your relationship with me will be that of conflict. If you get this, marriage will be a piece of cake. Remember, Anjali, men don't like complicated relationship. So, a man who is married to an alpha female, like in my case, is stuck between his willingness to please his wife and the desire to be incharge.'

'Did you ever feel this way?' enquired Anjali.

'Oh yes! I did,' replied Akhil with dismay. 'Many a time, I was pissed off and thought of committing suicide.'

'Really?' said Anjali, aghast.

'I am sorry, but yes. Though it was only a fleeting thought.'

'I feel so bad. I never thought my ambitions and dreams could have led to something as disastrous as that. I am relieved you didn't take such a step, Akhil,' replied Anjali, with moist eyes.

'Anjali, I have always been sensitive to your needs. Fortunately, a man's devotion to his wife is as strong as his devotion towards his own mother. Most men don't think about calling off their marriages until and unless it becomes unbearable. A noxious relationship in any form is you see what makes millions of unhappy faces around. I am glad that today you realized the importance of being a wife and most importantly, a woman. My dear wife, it is the dream of a man to return home to a peaceful environment. There is already a bundle of workload in office. To a man, his home represents a place where he can find peace and solace after the day's tiredness. Always remember that that two alphas never make a happy life. Most of the alpha males prefer betas which mean that betas are preferred more by men over alphas that are too difficult to handle, in comparison.'

'I get it now, Akhil. I wish I had understood these things earlier.'

'There is still a life ahead of us, dear. Focus on making things better at home rather than mourning over the past. We can still make efforts to improve the quality of life we live. The kids are growing now and we need to give them special attention. Anjali, prioritizing their needs will help you deal with them in a better way. But always remember the golden rule. Your family should be your first and the foremost priority. Rest all comes after that. I am happy that you finally understood. By the way, why this sudden change in your behaviour?'

'Well, I owe this to a man named Raunaq Ahuja.'

'Raunaq? Who is this? A new colleague?'

'No. He is an author of *Just Don't Do It*. I was so infuriated when I first read his book. He wrote so much about women that I didn't agree with. I even called him an anti-feminist when I met him today at Elena's birthday party. But I never though this words of wisdom would change my life forever. I am glad I met him.'

'Even I am.' There are very few who have such influential powers. He smiled and the two hugged each other.

15

Giving Is Not 'Giving Up'

Sitting on wooden chairs at one corner of the restaurant, the two smiled at each other.

'Thank you, Raunaq. Thank you for everything. I am sorry for being impolite the other day,' she said.

'You need not be, Anjali. There are many who curse me for my bluntness. You were just one of them,' he replied and she lowered her head.

'This is for you,' she said, handing him a copy of his book *Love in the Times of Jihad.* 'I want your autograph please.'

He smiled and said, 'So, how was it?'

'Oh! Everything between Akhil and me is back to normal now. I am glad we met.'

'I was talking about the book.' Raunaq grinned and the two let out a hearty laugh.

'Thank you, Raunaq. For everything that you did.'

'I didn't do anything, dear,' he said, smiling. 'It's you who decided to have a word with your husband and change for the better. I can only tell you how to live a better life. It's you who has to decide whether to act upon it or not, and I am glad you did!'

'I never thought that my relationship with Akhil would one day become so messed up. I know I was at fault, but I regret to say I didn't realize these things earlier. Yes, I loved him, but it is only recently that I have come to know and understand the true meaning of love. I feel bad when I look back now. All these years of my marriage had been a waste. It was only yesterday that I realized how adamant I have been.'

'Look, Anjali, whatever happened cannot be reversed. You cannot bring back the moments and chances that you have missed out on. But since you have realized now and feel sorry for them, the best you can do is to take charge of your relationship from now. And by saying that what I mean is that you need to focus on your family first rather than anything else. Rest all should be secondary in your life. Remember, Anjali, there is no better job in this world than taking care of your family. The corporate woman is more enslaved than the housewife because she is out of her powers and imitating male power is definitely not female power.'

'Yes. I understand. Akhil told me things that I had no clue about, feelings that I had paid no heed to in all these years running after power and position and facts that I had always turned a deaf ear to. You know, I once read a book by Dr Emerson Eggerichs, titled *Love & Respect*. I now understand the importance of the crazy cycle mentioned in it. Without respect, he reacts; without love, she reacts. It is all related. Dr Eggerichs had further mentioned wives are made to love, want to love and expect love, many husbands fail to deliver. It is just similar as the fact that husbands are made to be respected, want respect and expect respect, many wives fail to deliver.'

'True. Now you see what I meant to convey when I wrote that book?'

'Right. And this, I realized after talking to Akhil, yesterday. When a husband feels disrespected, it becomes especially hard for him to love his wife. In such a situation, he develops a natural tendency to react in ways that make her feel unloved. When a wife feels deprived of love, it becomes especially hard for her to respect her husband and she reacts in a way that seems disrespectful to her husband. In many cases, the wife's dislike is interpreted by the husband as disrespect and even contempt. If husbands and wives have to understand the love and respect connection, they must realize the importance of communication cannot be overemphasized. And the problem is that they don't know how to communicate with each other.'

'Very good, Anjali. You are talking sense now,' Raunaq beamed with delight. 'Well, on a serious note, I would rather live with a wife who respected me, but did not love me, than live with someone who loved me but did not respect me.'

'Respect is a man's most treasured value. A wife's sofetened tone and facial expressions can do wonders to solve conflicts in her marriage.'

'True. So what do you feel now? Raunaq enquired in a deep voice, looking straight into her eyes that glistened with tears in the dim light.

'I never knew I had stopped living,' replied Anjali. 'All this while, I had been running around like a machine, devoid of any emotions. What I felt yesterday was truly magical.

It felt like I had just woken up after a nightmare. Today, I realize the importance of my family, of being a wife and most importantly, the true meaning of women power. You have portrayed the homemaker as the noblest profession of this world. Even I agree to it now. The homemaker should be given the real credit for shaping society.'

'True. By and large, homemakers are the only ones who toil hard for their family. They are the ones who do not have regular time off. As a matter of fact, they go without a vacation for years. I personally feel that the job of a homemaker is quite strenuous. It is necessary that we do understand their importance and give them due credit for their efforts. Even married ladies today draw their inspiration from the single, independent women or the Bollywood beauties, which according to me is obnoxious.'

Anjali nodded her head in acknowledgement.

'Anjali, we are educating our children on every important aspect today. But what about the basics of a man–woman relationship? Don't you think it should be taught before the onset of adolescence? After all, relationship management is the core of every relationship. They even need to be educated about the differences between a man and a woman. It is not only physical but emotional as well.'

'You are right,' she said. 'Even my kids are growing up and I'll try to instill in them the basics of a healthy relationship. Do you know, Raunaq, I even told Akhil about you.'

'About me?'

'Yes. I told him that I have read your book and had criticized you for all that you have written.'

Raunaq smiled. 'That is not something new for me,' he said.

'Yes, what you have written in the book is actually a bit questionable at first. But if you explore the depths of it, the book does make sense. And so, I now want an autographed version of it,' Anjali smirked. 'It has changed my life and will be on the front row of my bookshelf from now on.'

Raunaq looked amused. He signed the book for her. She smiled back in return.

'By the way, I have resigned today.'

'Did you?' he questioned in disbelief.

'Yes. I have other important things to look after,' she said and the two exchanged smiles.

~

Two Years Later

It was two years since Raunaq and Anjali became friends. Akhil and Anjali were a happy couple. Even Arun and Rubina went along well. A lot had changed in all these years, but the thing that had drastically transformed was Anjali's behaviour. She had turned over a new leaf in the past two years and it was on Raunaq's request that she had agreed to come to this party today. It was Arun's fifth wedding anniversary. It was a beautiful evening with a huge gathering.

The venue was lit up with the beautiful moonlight. Draped in a bright-yellow saree, Anjali looked mesmerizing. It was the first time that she had chosen a traditional attire for an event. A small black bindi and a nude lip gloss complemented her looks. There were few who she knew at the party. Even Raunaq was nowhere to be seen. Feeling lost amidst the crowd, her eyes earnestly searched for someone to talk to.

'Anjali didi.' A silvery female voice from behind suddenly caught her attention and she turned around. The face seemed familiar, but she wasn't able to recognize who it was.

'Didi, it's me. Anu. Your friend Aradhya's younger sister. *Yaad aaya?* Do you remember?'

'Oh! Anu? What a pleasant surprise!' Anjali exclaimed. 'Where have you guys been all these years and where is Aradhya? How is she? And what are you doing here in this party?'

'Relax, didi,' Anu smiled. 'This is my party. It is my anniversary today,' she said.

'Your anniversary? You mean to say you are Arun's wife?'

'Yes. I am and it's our anniversary party.'

'Oh! Congratulations. Actually I came here on the invitation from a common friend, Raunaq.'

'Yes, I know him. Raunaq Ahuja. He was Arun's colleague and they are close friends too.'

'Yes. Right!'

'Oh! But I am so glad to see you today. It has been long since we saw or heard from you.'

'Same here. I never knew we were in the same city. Where is Aradhya?' Anjali enquired.

'She is inside. Please come in,' Anu said, directing Anjali towards the massive hall. She stopped behind a woman of their age who was preoccupied with the other guests. 'Aradhya di, look who is here!' Anu exclaimed with childlike enthusiasm. The girl turned around and the three of them shrieked out together.

'Anjali!' Aradhya cried out. 'What a surprise! Where have you been all these years?'

'Surprisingly, in the same city,' Anjali replied.

'What? Really? And we never met. How unfortunate!'

'Yes. It is. Had I not come here, I would have never known about you being in the same city.'

'Really!' Aradhya exclaimed. 'You know what? Barkha and I have been looking for you since ages. And you meet me like this! What a surprise it is!'

'Barkha? Are you both in touch? How is she?' said Anjali, surprised.

'Oh yes. We are in touch and she is doing good,' Aradhya replied. 'She is working in a top position for a company in Gurgaon. Actually, we met after ages at an award function. That was also a coincidence. We both were nominated for the Women Achievers Award and I met her after the ceremony. Since then, we have regularly been in touch.'

'That's great! It feels so nice to meet you. And I hope to see Barkha soon!'

'Yes. We'll plan something soon. By the way, what are you doing nowadays? You were the topper of our college. I believe you have a high-paying job.'

Anjali smiled. 'No, I am a housewife.'

'A housewife?' Anjali's unexpected reaction shook Aradhya a little.

'Yes. A housewife and I am pretty satisfied with my job.' Anjali was firm in whatever she said.

'You call it a job?' Aradhya looked at Anjali, amused.

'Yes. Why not? In fact, it is the noblest profession in this world.'

'Profession? Well, my dear. I call it slavery.' Aradhya smirked a little. 'You have become a slave to your husband. What happened to you, Anjali? You have curbed your freedom for the sake of a man. That's pathetic! Who gave you this advice? Look at us. We are living a life of dignity sans any nuisance. I feel sorry for you.'

'I know, Aradhya, how you must be feeling. Yes, I had a job and a decent one too. But I left it all, to look after my family. Today, I am happy with what I am doing and this may surprise you, but I have no regrets. Anyway, you tell me. How are you and Ravi? I am sorry I couldn't attend your wedding.'

'Ravi is no more, Anjali. He succumbed to a major heart attack years ago. Now I have two little daughters who mean the world to me,' replied Aradhya with dismay.

'Oh! I am sorry to hear that.'

'No. It's okay. It's been years now. I have a government job in hand.'

'That's really nice. But as far as I know, you were never interested in a job. Living a simple, carefree life was the only thing that you craved for. It's a surprise that you are a working woman now,' said Anjali.

'Hmm. Circumstances, dear. I was left with no other option after Ravi's demise. And now, I am a confident woman.'

'That's good. By the way, where is Arun?'

'God knows where he is. If Ravi were alive, he would have never left us alone in a party. You know, Anjali, Ravi used to say that a person who does not drink is khadoos and I must say that Arun is also khadoos. I am sorry to say that Arun is a man who has no control over his own actions,' replied Aradhya.

'God knows how Anu tolerates that man? If I was in her place, I would have left him a long time back,' the often-repeated dialogue of Aradhya followed.

'Yes, Anjali didi. Aradhyadi is absolutely right. Arun is such a negative man,' commented Anu, who was listening to the entire conversation. 'He is not at all like Ravi jiju. I know he must be sulking somewhere in the remotest corner of the house.'

'Don't you think you need to be with him today? After all, it's your anniversary, Anu,' Anjali replied.

'Why should I care for a man who cannot take care of himself, didi? Do you know, Ravi jiju was so different? He supported Aradhya di, at all times. Even at parties, he would walk around holding hands with her. Arun is not at all like him. He is a jerk.'

'All men are jerks, Anu,' Aradhya replied.

'Why? Was even Ravi like that?' Anjali questioned. The unexpected comment from Aradhya had left her bewildered.

'No. Ravi was a great man. In fact, he was out of this world. He was not at all like the others.'

'I agree and I wish Arun was like him,' Anu sighed.

Anjali chose to remain silent. It was for the first time that she understood the reason behind Arun's resentment and distress. The first time they had met, she barely knew the facts but now, it was all crystal clear to her.

'Accha, Aradhya. I have to leave now. My family must

be waiting for me. I told them it wouldn't take long. Please do wish Arun from my side and I'll catch up with you some other time. Say hi to Barkha.'

'Sure. It was a pleasure meeting you, dear,' replied Aradhya, hugging her tight.

'Same here. We'll meet soon.'

The two quickly exchanged numbers and Anjali waved goodbye to Aradhya with a promise to catch up at the earliest.

16

No Man Is an Island

It was not long after Arun and Anu's anniversary party that Aradhya received a call from Barkha.

'Barkha,' Aradhya replied breathlessly. 'I am glad you called, dear. In fact, I was just about to give you a call.'

'Wait, wait. Hold on, sweetheart. What got you so excited?'

'Umm, I have a surprise for you.'

'For me?' asked Barkha, inquisitively.

'Yes. For you!'

'Tell me then.'

'Not now. I'll tell you when we meet next.'

'As a matter of fact, I called you up to tell that my flight has just landed in Lucknow. So, can we plan a meet in a day or two?'

'What?' Aradhya asked, her heart beating faster. 'You are in Lucknow! Oh, I can't tell you how excited I am.'

The excitement in Aradhya's voice puzzled Barkha and she replied rolling her eyes, 'You are causing quite a stir now! What is it? Come on spill the beans please!'

'Okay, okay. I'll tell you, if you insist. I have found Anju, finally!' revealed Aradhya.

'What! How? When? Where?'

'Hold on, hold on, Barkha. I'll tell you everything when we meet. Right now, I'll call her up and tell her about our meeting!'

'Oh, I am so excited to see her. It's been long since we three met.'

'Right. But you'll be surprised to know that she has transformed into a housewife these days.'

'Are you kidding me?'

'Absolutely not, Barkha. Why would I? I am serious. Even I was shocked when she told me about it.'

'Okay, that sounds interesting. Can we meet tomorrow at 1.00 p.m. at Fun Republic Mall? Will that be okay?'

'Perfect!'

The euphoria of reunion filled her heart and she wished the day would slip away soon!

Aradhya kept the receiver, feeling delighted and immediately called up Anjali to share the news with her.

ஐ

At around 1 p.m., the three—Anjali, Barkha and Aradhya—met at the entrance gate of the mall. All three of them were together after what felt like ages. Their faces lit up with smiles. Needless to say, they got nostalgic. Hugging each other merrily, they made their way towards the mall. The chatters, the giggles and even the lame jokes that they cracked, everything was spontaneous, just like old times. They were pumped with excitement.

'Oh! I am so happy to see you, Anju,' exclaimed Barkha. 'You know how excited I have been since Aradhya told me about meeting you.'

'Same here. You know, we met at Anu's anniversary party and I had no clue who the host was,' Anjali winked at Aradhya.

'Really?'

'Yes, really! It was an invitation from a common friend.'

'That's cool! I guess we were destined to meet. Meeting Aradhya was also a coincidence for us,' Barkha said with the wink of an eye.

'Yes, she told me all about it. It seems like a decade, na?'

'Right. I missed this togetherness like anything.'

'Me too. So, where are you working these days? Aradhya told me you are in a prominent company in Gurgaon.'

'Oh yes. I am working with Fashionista Ventures Private Limited,' replied Barkha.

'Wow! That's a renowned name in the fashion industry.'

'Yes, it is. I was the CEO of the company till I lost that position to a bitch.'

'Oh! I am sorry to hear that. But may I know the reason?'

'Nothing new, yaar. These newcomers, they use the boss as a ladder for promotion and success. She did the same and snatched my position. She is a fox…' Barkha rolled her eyes in exasperation.

'Don't forget, you used the same trick,' interfered Aradhya. 'You cannot blame the girl? Yes, I agree it feels dreadful.'

'Did you?' said Anjali, fixing her gaze upon Barkha, 'That was least expected of you.'

'Oh! C'mon Anju, don't be a preacher. Everyone does

it and so have I. What's wrong in it? You have to sacrifice something in order to be successful. Everyone is not a topper like you. And please don't behave like Aneesh,' Barka lashed out at Anjali, who stared at her in dismay. 'Aneesh?' she questioned.

'Yes. Aneesh, my husband. I am so fed up of him. He keeps on finding ways to criticize me.'

'And why do think so?' retorted Anjali.

'I do not think so, Anju. This is a fact. I have a messed up marital life. Anyway, leave all this. You tell me, Aradhya was telling me that you have resorted to being a housewife. How degrading is that! With all the professional degrees that you have, you chose to be a homemaker. How in the world do you justify that?'

'That is exactly what I have been wondering too, Anju,' added Aradhya. 'Why a mere housewife, when you could have easily got a hefty-paying job?'

'Relax, both of you,' Anjali replied. 'I know you have many questions and I promise to answer all before we leave today. First of all, let me tell you something. Being a housewife is not a piece of cake. Yes, I have turned into one and I admit there is no better job.'

'So, do you mean to say that we should all leave our jobs and become housewives?'

'No, I am not saying that. It's your life and ultimately, your decision. I cannot force anything on you. I can only share my experiences with you,' said Anjali.

'Aradhya, you tell me. What were you saying about Arun that night?'

'Arun? Oh, only that he is a good-for-nothing husband.

There's nothing more to say about him,' Aradhya replied.

'Good for nothing? Why?'

'You don't know, Anju. He cannot keep my sister happy. Ravi was just the opposite. He was a perfect man, a perfect husband, a perfect father, a perfect son and a perfect son-in-law. Arun comes nowhere close.'

'So, do you mean that Ravi is the new definition of "perfect"?'

'I did not say that,' Aradhya protested.

'But it seems so…at least from what you just said. Tell me, Aradhya, are you perfect? Is Anu perfect? Well, according to me, no one is perfect. Even God has His own imperfections. And we are just humans. Why do you run after perfection? Aradhya, try to judge less and love more. If you avoid people for their little mistakes, you will always be alone. You are saying that Arun cannot keep his wife happy. Then why did he choose to live next to you people? He could have lived with his parents. It was Anu, I guess who wanted to live near you. Correct me if I am wrong.'

'No…but…'

'Have you ever noticed the little things that he does for his wife to keep her happy? Well, I don't think that you or your sister has ever observed that. Aradhya, everyone has issues. You never know what people are going through. So, think before you start judging, mocking or criticizing anyone. It is a fact, Aradhya, that every husband wants his wife to be happy. He can do anything to please her and this is what I have realized from my own experiences in life. You seem to belittle Arun and his efforts every time and in front of everyone. Even at the party, you never once thought about him. Have you ever wondered how he must have felt? Not only that, you are even polluting Anu's mind and compelling her to believe that her husband is good for nothing. In spite of all this, Arun is with you and your sister. I think he really deserves a big applause for that.'

'Anju, I have not polluted my sister's mind. She herself told me that Arun doesn't love her. Now what do you have to say about that?'

'Aradhya, to love means to give. The most elementary example lies in the sphere of sex. A man gives himself to a woman. He even gives his semen at the moment of orgasm. For a woman, the process is not different. She gives herself too. In the act of receiving, she offers herself. She gives herself to the growing child within her, she nurses the infant and provides it with love and warmth. Don't you think not to give would be painful? As far as Arun is concerned, I guess he has given his all to this relationship. Ask Anu if she has ever respected her husband as an individual? You people keep on comparing Arun with Ravi, who unfortunately is no more. What did Anu say that night? Even at parties, Ravi jiju used to walk holding hands with Aradhya di. Am I right?'

'Hmm.' Aradhya nodded in approval.

'Aradhya, not every man believes in PDA. There are many who do not prefer such public display of affection. But that doesn't necessarily mean that they are emotionless. Of course, Arun has emotions too. He loves Anu a lot and I have seen it in his eyes. Let me share with you an interesting fact. Do share this with Anu as well. Aradhya, a man needs to be respected as much as a woman needs to be loved. No husband will feel affectionate if he believes that his wife has contempt for him. You can say that the deepest need of a woman, that is to feel loved, is undermined by her disrespect for her husband. And it's not wrong. This is what Anu has been doing to her husband all this while. I must say that she is the one who is responsible for her loveless married life. This happens, Aradhya, when a wife does not show respect towards the husband. The husband then gradually ceases to love his wife. After all, who wants to keep talking to someone who doesn't know your language?'

'You are talking about things that we have never heard of, Anju,' retorted Barkha. 'I do not know much about this male–female ideology but all I know is that even my husband is a jerk. Not only Arun, but even Aneesh is a looser. I am an independent woman and I want my partner to be equal to me, in all respect.

'Barkha, what is this "equality" that you are talking about? This is only an artificial environment that we have created for ourselves. However, both men and women desire different things when it comes to sex and love. Not better, nor worse, but different! Barkha, what women of the twenty-first century really want in men are the basic things that their ancestral mothers once asked for and that is good hunting skills and resources needed to provide them with food. Apart from this, they wanted the male to look after them and their family. Even today's women crave for such basics. They want men who have money, good education, status, authority and a sense of humour, all of which is an indicator of good resources. Even the female criterion for an eligible bachelor is a man who has these resources. Equality today means sameness rather than oneness.'

'So is there something wrong in it? Even men want something from us,' Barkha replied.

'Oh yes, they do! The same thing applies to the other sex as well. A twenty-first century man looks for the same things in a woman as his forefathers and that is her ability to successfully carry forward his genes and to nurture him and their offspring. As I already said, respect is the thing that men crave for the most. Barkha, men look for emotional support in a serious relationship rather than anything else. Men, as far as I have understood, only want few basic things from their wives. These are physical intimacy, good food, house, to be loved and respected. It's that simple. They don't have complicated demands that we have. The only problem today is that what's more important to a man is likely to be seen as the thing of the least priority by women and vice versa. But we have not been able to understand that.'

'Anju, do you mean that there is some error in communication? A misunderstanding?'

'Yes, of course! If a husband and wife are to understand each other, and for love and respect to grow between them, they must be able to decode their communication. The problem is that they do not know how to decipher the communication. Men and women look at the same situation through different glasses. And by that I mean through different perspectives. You just need to understand it. But again, there's a problem. No one wants to change. Right? We do not want to compromise at any level. Don't want to change yourself for anyone else. How many times have we heard this narrative?'

'Yes, we have heard that. And I totally agree to it,' said Aradhya. 'Why do you need to change yourself for anyone in this world? If someone really loves you, he'll love you the way you are. And why compromise in a relationship? According to me, a relationship that requires you to compromise is unreal and not worth being in,' she said.

'Well, Aradhya. I think differently. I believe that sometimes changing yourself is the positive sign in order to improve a relationship. In fact, changing yourself with the times and according to the demands of your relationship is absolutely necessary. Relationships are based on compromises. There will always be awkward angles and sharp edges between you and your partner that you need to ease out in order to fit together as a strong seamless unit. Two people who wish to have any sort of relationship between them need to compromise, at some or the other stage. You cannot win every argument that triggers between you and your husband. The most important thing here is to understand that every trivial argument is not a battle. Reluctance to compromise leads to the breakdown of relationships and eventually of families today.'

'Aradhya, you have no right to say such a thing,' said Barkha. 'Remember, you once told me that you tasted non-veg food for Ravi. Just because Ravi wanted you to do so. You could have easily avoided having it but no, you chose to surrender. Why? It was just forty-eight hours of your togetherness then and you took a lifelong decision to give in to his likes and dislikes. Just because you are independent now doesn't mean that you forget all that you did in the past. You have enjoyed marital bliss because you made sacrifices. I think Anju is right. You should not teach Anu to disrespect her husband's side of the family. Who knows how Ravi would have been if he were alive. He was in his twenties when he passed away and Arun is in his thirties. You cannot compare two men with that much of an age difference. Not only that, I think even your daughters will get a negative vibe from you. They'll never understand the importance of being in a relationship.'

Barkha looked at Aradhya as she remembered those days, those eyes and a lot more. It had been a small two-room house that Aradhya's family lived in and they were a big family. Aradhya, her sister, Anu and brother, Somesh, shared one room whilst the other was reserved for their parents. There was a small area outside the rooms that was crammed with household items. It was a cosy place for the family to dwell in until Aradhya got married. Her husband, Ravi, was an army officer who used to stay out on field postings most of the time. But he visited them on a regular basis. Being a newly married couple, the duo craved for some privacy during the night hours, which never seemed possible because of frequent interruption from the others.

'This is not done, Aradhya,' Ravi had said, one cold night, his voice curt. 'I come here only for a couple of days, but you never seem to have time for me. You are too busy pleasing everyone else.'

Aradhya had never heard such words from Ravi. This dejection coming from him made her shiver and she replied meekly, 'I am yours, Ravi. Tell me where did I go wrong?'

'It's not about being wrong or right, Aradhya. I am never able to make love to my wife, just because we are so crowded by everyone else. I also have some needs to be fulfilled and you being a wife should take care of that,' Ravi had retorted sulkily.

Aradhya lovingly cupped his face in her hands and replied, 'I promise, we'll have a good time tonight.' She placed her finger on his lips and kissed it sensually looking deep into his eyes. Holding her hands firmly in a tight grip, he planted a soft kiss on her collarbone, 'I'll wait for you,' he said.

That night was the best that Aradhya had with Ravi. It was full of thrill and excitement. It had been the first time that she had escaped her family to make love to Ravi, on the terrace, under the starlit sky. Just in case no one woke up to find her missing, she had bolted the rooms from outside and had quickly tiptoed upstairs where Ravi had been waiting for her eagerly.

'Oh! I have been waiting for this moment since morning,' he had said, hugging her and his hands exploring her back over the satin night wear that she wore.

'Ravi!' she had whispered. He didn't hear her and had continued to take off her dress wildly. After exposing her to the bare minimum, he had removed his shirt and had unhooked her bra with a grin. All that while, his lips and fingers had continued to explore her insanely.

'Will you remove the rest yourself or do you want me to do the honours?' he had whispered, sucking her earlobes. Hungry for more, Aradhya had lifted her hips a little and he had swiftly tugged out her underwear, and she had stood nude on the isolated terrace.

He had circled her nipples with his lips and she moaned in pleasure. The cool breeze had brushed against her breasts, making her shiver. The frequent kisses that he had planted on her collarbone, chin and lips, elevated Aradhya's sexual desires that she had kept bottled up for days.

'You are wet!' he had said, exploring deep down with his fingers.

'No, I am all soaked,' she whispered as Ravi made desperate attempts to nibble her earlobes. With one hand resting on her hips, he slapped her butt cheek with the other making her shriek in pain. Their eyes met when he inserted a finger inside her and she winced. 'Please be careful,' she said coyly, closing her eyes at every move that he made.

She kissed him back as the intensity of the act grew. She stroked his erection till the time he finally entered her, making her moan with excitement. She remembered it hurting but the pleasure was far beyond the pain and she had enjoyed all that was happening.

'Does it feel good?' he asked.

She nodded in contentment, her eyes still closed. Within few minutes, she had moaned out loud and the two lay next to each other, his fingers exploring her deep navel. She had covered her face with embarrassment as he gently squeezed her breasts.

'How do you feel?' Ravi asked.

'Complete,' she answered, covering her face.

'I love you,' he whispered, planting a soft kiss on her forehead.

'I love you too,' she replied back promptly.

That day, as far as Aradhya could remember they have had one of the best steaming orgasms of all times. It was an adventure sex for the couple that increased the excitement levels by leaps and bounds. This continued for days until one day Ravi suggested to make love in the small washroom that was connected to the common area of the house. Aradhya had been hesitant, but one day when her younger brother and sister were away, she decided to give it a try. Carefully, she tiptoed to the washroom where Ravi had been waiting for her desperately.

'I knew you'll come,' he whispered, nibbling her earlobe. She kissed him back gently as he lifted her up in his arms and unhooked her bra. As the two were about to get swayed away by the ocean of desires, a known voice from outside disturbed their act.

'Aradhya,' her mother called from outside.

'Oh no,' she murmured, nervously placing a hand on her mouth. Even Ravi stood still as the voice came closer. 'Are you inside?' her mother called.

'Yes, Mom. I am taking a shower. Just give me five minutes.'

'Where is Ravi?'

'I don't know, Mom. He left the house a little while ago. Maybe he is on some important call.'

'Okay. Come out fast. I am serving lunch.'

'Five minutes please, Mom,' Aradhya replied, trying to loosen Ravi's strong grip. 'Leave me, Ravi. Mom can be here anytime soon. I don't want her to catch us like this.'

'Tell her you need some more time in the shower,' he replied caressing her silky shoulder-length hair with one hand and rubbing over her brassiere with the other. She whined feebly as he began lifting her dress to expose her deep sexy navel and circled it with his fingers. She had started liking the way he licked her, making her go wet. He kissed her passionately and she reciprocated with soft cries that were drowned by the sound of running water.

'How much more time, Aradhya?' her mother called from outside.

'Five more minutes, please,' she managed to fumble while Ravi sucked her bare breasts. Not being able to control herself for long, she removed his wet t-shirt and shorts, and climbed on top of him, giving him the ride of a lifetime. Having reached her climax, Aradhya quickly took a shower and towel-dried herself. She then peeped out of the washroom to check if everything was okay and then headed straight to her room. She hurriedly changed into a new dress before heading towards the kitchen for lunch. Ravi, who managed to step out noiselessly, joined the family after a while. The two winked at each other at the table whilst the others were busy having their lunch.

These quick sessions that the couple indulged in, sneaking out while the family was away or asleep, brought them closer bit by bit, day by day.

∾

Aradhya vividly remembered all of it, as if it was all happening in front of her eyes and she could still feel a tickling sensation as the memories came to mind.

'True, Barkha. I am glad you understood my point,' said Anjali, snapping her fingers at Aradhya, thus bringing her back to reality.

'Well, I must admit, Anju. It's a valid one!' admitted Barkha softly.

'Aradhya,' said Anjali. 'You are planting the seeds of independence in Anu and your kids. Why don't you understand that not everyone in this world will end up being a widow or land up in a failed relationship? I agree that life is full of illusions and death is the ultimate truth, but we need to teach our children to live a happy life and not to live in the past. Aradhya, stop crafting your life and your family's around "those who are dead". The very essence of your personality lies in your ideas, emotions and prejudices. We should wipe out all our memories and embrace life, the present. You are always living in your memory, you are essentially investing in the dead. You are an undertaker, your business is with the dead all the time.'

'I do not agree with what you are saying,' Aradhya said red-faced. 'But, Anju, I believe that everything is a fight and unless it is highly opportune to say yes, is it necessary to surrender?'

'But that is what you had done in your past,' replied Anjali. 'Unconditional love and sacrifices were eventually the elements that made your marital life a success. You may not realize this now because you don't even realize that you have undergone a complete transformation in all these years. My dear lady, a husband is responsible for his own actions but his behaviour is inextricably linked to that of his wife. And this is the reason why Ravi had been great. It's because you chose to surrender for the sake of your relationship. It was perhaps for only twelve years, but you did enjoy marital bliss. In that case, aren't you misguiding Anu? Aradhya, what I believe is that it takes a great deal of effort and discipline to have a blissful married life. You should actually prepare your sister for that. Can you please explain why does she have to stay away from her in-laws?'

'It's because they do not share a cordial relationship. Her

views do not match her mother-in-law's,' Aradhya replied.

'Aradhya, ask Anu if she has genuinely tried to improve her relationship with her in-laws. They are her family, just like you all. Ask her if she has ever asked Arun to fight with his parents for her and then tell me whether that is justified. What if I ask Anu to fight with you for Arun? Will she happily do that? Just think about it. In many cases, we find that husbands who do not stand up for their wives often end up destroying their marriages. Tell me, Aradhya, why do men need to fight with their families to please their wives? Have you ever asked Ravi to fight for you? And do you think Ravi would have ever tolerated if you would have asked him to.'

Aradhya sat still. She had no answers to Anjali's questions. Even Barkha chose to remain quiet. Anjali continued, 'Let me share something with you. I have left my job as the vice president of a company.'

Anjali took a pause as both Barkha and Aradhya gaped at her in astonishment. 'I had everything. Money, power, position, success, everything. But what I lacked was mental peace. I never enjoyed a blissful married life. Akhil was disturbed and so were our children. Then I met Raunaq.'

'Raunaq Ahuja?' Aradhya questioned.

'Yes. The same Raunaq. I shared my thoughts and views with him and he made me realize how wrong I have been all throughout my life. At first, I refused to surrender to his thoughts, just like you two. But then, I realized that he was right. It's been two years since I followed his advice and today I am a housewife. I have a happy husband, two happy kids who are growing up in a carefree environment and a happy family. I do not have regrets because the happiness that I am enjoying being a beta female is worth all the sacrifices.

'Aradhya, you know I watched a discourse by Sadhguru on Youtube in which he clearly stated that human relations are always variable. If you want to have an absolute relationship, you can have a relationship either with the dead or God. You have a relationship with a dead person. Don't transfer this to your family. When you are in a relationship with God, you don't think about God for ten days and on the eleventh day God is there, but in human relationships that is not possible, human relationships need a lot of energy and investment. If you got busy for three years and then you think about God or a dead person, they are still there. So prepare your children for human relationships.'

It was a conversation that took up the entire evening. While Aradhya reminisced about her life with Ravi, Barkha wondered what had gone wrong between her and Aneesh.

'It's already late,' Anjali said, looking at her watch. 'We need to leave now.'

'When are we going to meet next?' asked Barkha.

'Anytime soon!' Anjali replied, grinning.

'Anju…' said Aradhya.

'Hmm.'

'Thank you for this evening.'

'Why?'

'No one has been able to show us the mirror, the way you did today. I am glad we met.'

'Aradhya, as I already said. I can only share my experiences. To change or not to change is entirely up to you. I am glad you understood,' Anjali replied and the three hugged each other.

17

It's Him and I

Sometimes our lives have to be completely shaken, changed and rearranged to relocate us to the place we are meant to be at. There are times when the only way to improve our lives is to force ourselves to undergo a complete change and this might mean leaving behind a dysfunctional relationship, leaving a high-paying and secure job or something else. Even Barkha and Aradhya had gone through a transformation after meeting Anjali that day after a long time.

A Month Later

It was a scorching Sunday afternoon when both Akhil and Anjali were busy discussing issues related to his office. The children were not at home and the couple was having a pleasurable time together.

'Anju,' said Akhil lovingly, cupping her face in his hands. 'You have changed a lot. And I feel so relieved now. You know what, I have always missed these moments, these moments when we would sit together and talk. But things were so different in between. You were either working late hours or you were extremely fatigued at the end of the day. I never really got a chance to share my feelings with you. And I'll tell you something else. When your husband comes to you with a problem, he wants you to listen to him and not to retaliate.'

'I know, Akhil, the last two years have been very special for me, for us and for our relationship. I agree that not all changes are bad!' She winked at him.

Akhil kissed Anjali's forehead and said, 'I feel relaxed when I come back home in the evening. Actually, it feels good to see you with a smile. You know something, dear, men like calmness. The husband wants to come home at the end of the day to a peaceful environment. To him, home represents a place of refuge. For wives, I guess it is more than that. As a female, you're more invested in it.'

'I agree with you, Akhil. Actually I have lived both the lives—that of a working woman as well as that of a homemaker. I feel now that working is about making money and having power, whereas marriage is about love. If you want to be successful in both, you need to know how to switch gears and surrender to love at home.'

'I am glad you understood this fact. Life seems to be back on track again,' Akhil said, holding her in his arms. While he planted a soft kiss on her cheeks, she tightly wrapped her hands around his waist.

Suddenly, there was a ring on their landline phone which broke the beautiful embrace they were in.

'Hello!' Anjali said picking up the receiver.

'Hello, Anju,' a female voice at the other end of the

receiver greeted her graciously. It was Aradhya.

'Hey! Hello, Aradhya. How have you been?'

'I am doing great, dear. Accha listen, I have an invitation for you and Akhil.'

'Invitation?'

'Yes'

'Whose invite is it?'

'Mine,' Aradhya giggled. 'I am hosting a party tonight and you both are invited. It's important and I do not want to hear a no.'

'Alright, alright. I won't say no. But will you tell me what occasion it is?'

'That's a surprise. You'll come to know when you reach here. I am hanging up now and remember, its sharp 6. I'll message you about the venue. Don't be late.'

~

Unaware of the occasion Aradhya was celebrating, Anjali reached the venue along with Akhil. It was difficult for her to persuade him to come along as they did not know why they were invited.

'Will you clear the suspense, Anjali?' asked Akhil impatiently.

'Even I am not aware of the occasion, dear husband. Please have patience. I guess it must be something grand!' Anjali replied, pinching him playfully.

He smiled, she smiled and the two hugged each other.

'I love you,' he said.

'I love you too.'

Together they made their way towards the entrance of

the five-star hotel that was beautifully decorated with red and white satin ribbons and balloons. There was a huge gathering that included common friends, hot shots and mediapersons.

'Anju!' Akhil whispered as they took a seat somewhere in the middle of the hall. 'Are you sure we are at the right place? I mean, there's such a huge gathering here and surprisingly we don't even know the reason for this party!'

'I can make out a few of the faces. They belong to the filthy rich segment of the society. There are even a few of the mediapersons whom I personally know,' replied Anjali, exchanging quick smiles with a guy at a distance.

'Hey, Anjali,' greeted a familiar voice from behind. It was Raunaq.

'Hey, Raunaq,' Anjali waved him back and gestured him to have a seat next to them. Needless to say she was more than happy to meet him. 'What is this party about? Do you have any idea?' she asked him. 'Barkha and Aradhya didn't tell me anything. Do you have a clue?'

Raunaq nodded in affirmation. 'Yes, I know and you'll soon get to know too.'

'Please, Raunaq. I feel left out and it really feels strange to not know the occasion of a party that you are attending. Please spill the beans...' she protested, but before Raunaq could speak further, a call from a lady on the decorated stage caught their attention.

'Hello everyone!' she addressed in a high-pitched tone. 'My name is Purabi Roy and I am your host for the evening. Two lovely ladies whom I met years back in an award function, Mrs Barkha Malhotra and Mrs Aradhya Sharma, are the organizers of this party and this evening is dedicated to someone very special in their lives. And I guess the person for whom we all have been waiting all this while has arrived. Mrs Anjali Mathur, will you grace the stage with your presence?'

Anjali turned her head to see if there was any other Anjali Mathur in the party.

'Mrs Anjali Mathur, can we please have you on stage?'

Clearly there was no other Anjali Mathur at the party and therefore, Anjali stood up rather hesitatingly and started walking towards the stage. One look at Raunaq and she knew that he knew what was happening!

'Thank you, Mrs Mathur,' greeted Purabi and they both exchanged quick smiles. 'You must be wondering the reason for this affair! So, without any further delay, I would like to call upon Mrs Barkha and Mrs Aradhya on stage along with Mr Raunaq Ahuja.'

A little while later, the three turned up on stage, smiling.

'I know you must be puzzled, Anjali,' chuckled Barkha, holding hands with her.

Meanwhile, Purabi handed over the mike to Aradhya, who stood at a distance with a smile on her face.

'I know it sounds weird when I say that this celebration is for the change that has drastically changed our lives. To some, I may sound insane, but those who know the story behind this will understand how important it is for us to share this feeling with you all. I am not ashamed to say that I am good for nothing. I have never been a good sister, a good daughter-in-law or even a good mother. But this was months back until I met her.' Aradhya said pointing out to Anjali, who gaped at her in astonishment.

'Life was good for me as an alpha female. I was independent. I was ambitious. I was rich. But I had never been successful in terms of my relationships. They had always been a disaster. When I met Anjali a few months back, I didn't know this would happen. The realization and the subsequent transformation from being an alpha to a beta female has not been easy. Accomplishing anything great in life requires effort and significant change that pushes us beyond our comfort zones. Even we had problems, but I am glad we have changed,' Aradhya said, looking joyously at Barkha, who smiled back in support. 'Today when I look back, I find ashes of my past that fortunately I have been able to leave behind. This is wonderful, this life, this world. Everything seems to be beautiful about being a beta female. It is all perfect. My family has suffered a lot because of my ignorant behaviour in the past. I would like to call upon my sister Anu here. She has something really important to confess and trust me, before we begin with anything else, it's important to know this part of the story as well.'

Anu, who was seated a distance from the stage, came on stage and took the mike from her. 'I confess that I had been a fool till date. My husband is really nice, but I compared him with someone who is not even in this world now. I used to think like others and follow the path led by my sister. But now, I know the true worth of this relationship. My husband has been by my side through thick and thin and though I am late in confessing it, I love and respect him for all that he has done for me and my family. I have completely understood that at the end, it's only me and him. No one has the right to meddle in my relationship. And by no one I mean *no one*, not even my sister. There are women who talk about feminism, but they are not actually concerned about the whole community. They are those who feel inferior as compared to the rest. They wish to rearrange this society, just like my sister Aradhya did. Just because she is single, she wants to change everything around her. These feminists will tell you anything to prove their point. Please don't get carried away by all these talks. In the name of feminism, you are being served notions that will destroy your relationships forever. There'll be no one to share your sorrows and pain. It's only your husband who's going to stand by you. At the end, only you and your husband are going to stay forever. So think wisely before it's too late. And I request Aradhya to find someone and settle down in life because society is based on family and having a family is great.' Anu sobbed as she spoke. She further handed the mike to Barkha, who hugged her back.

'Let me brief you about our story,' continued Barkha. 'And by our, I mean Aradhya and me. We were the kind of women who could do anything for the sake of our work. We were independent and ambitious. But an important element in our lives was missing and this, we realized when we met Anjali. For those who do not know her, let me tell you, she's the best friend we've ever had. The importance of family and relationships were overruled by ambitions in our lives. When we are talking about relationships, I'll share my take on it with you all. Well, to make or destroy a relationship is ultimately the decision of the partners. But we are so busy playing the blame game that we eventually turn a blind eye to our preferences. There are not many who understand the concepts of love and respect. The female desire to be loved and the male desire to feel respected are the ultimate bases for any relationship. Without respect, there'll be no love. We fail to understand this simple logic and unfortunately we even groom our children in this direction. What we ignore, is the fact that relationships are based on compromises. Say for example, your interests and hobbies may vary. Obviously you cannot leave all your interests to be in a relationship, but it's only natural that the more time you spend with your partner, the more invested you become in their likes and dislikes. So, you see there can be different ways to look at a situation or conflict. I totally agree with what Anu has just said. This is perhaps the biggest truth of life. At the end, when there'll be no one to hold you back, you'll only find solace in the arms of your partner. Because ultimately, it will be only Him and I.'

'Mr Ahuja,' said Purabi handing over the mike to Raunaq. 'You have written a book about relationships. What do you have to say about this whole realization?'

'Actually, Purabi, there's a lot that I can tell you about relationships. Not only Barkha and Aradhya but there are many women in this world who are striving hard to be independent and successful. And as per my observations, learning how to drive is the first step towards asserting their independence for them. In fact, it wouldn't be wrong if I say that single women are obsessed with driving. You can find plenty of such females on streets who actually drive with frustration. Just because they are single, they want to run everyone down. And out of these, there are many who don't even know the essence of love,' replied Raunaq and smiled wryly at her.

Purabi raised her brows and asked, 'Will you please explain this?'

'Purabi, I believe that to love means to serve. It's something you give and not something you get. As far as the relationship between a man and a woman is concerned, let me tell you that men are programmed to serve the women they love. They love to please their wives in every possible manner. Whereas, the women in India are now being groomed to never adhere to men's likes and dislikes. The alpha female tends to live according to her needs and plans, not her husband's.'

'But alpha women are independent,' retorted Purabi.

'Independent at what cost? Is it for free? Or is it at the cost of their relationships? Purabi, it is not only the single women who are destroying their relationships in their greed for more, but I regretfully say that even the married ones are looking at them in awe and are unfortunately drawing their inspiration from them. Just have a look at these movie stars or the page 3 women, and if you happen to have a sneak peek behind their glamorous faces, you'll find that they earn their living by selling their conscience. What I believe is that a woman should make a homemaker as her point of reference, rather than those who belong to the world of glitz and glamour. Learn from them. Respect them and see what sacrifices they have made to keep their families intact. And I am sure you'll understand what all it takes to keep someone happy. Well, if you ask me, I would say that a homemaker holds the highest value in comparison to any other woman in this world.'

Purabi looked bemused and baffled at Raunaq's reply, she questioned further, 'Just look at me, Mr Raunaq, I am independent and I am happy about it. I don't want to commit myself to a relationship and become a slave for my entire life. Marriage is bondage for me. What is your say on it?'

'Well, Purabi, that's entirely your choice. But my say on marriage is a little different. I believe that it provides ample benefits to women as compared to men, though you may or may not realize. Anything goes wrong and you have the entire world supporting you. But men, they are never supposed to be crybabies. If a woman decides to leave a guy, she has all the right to do so without losing her children or without being financially weak. But what do men have? Nothing. In fact, they need to pay alimony. It's obvious that he has to forget about his wife and children, though he might not have wanted the separation. For every trivial marital issue, the law provides protection to women but what about men, Purabi? Where do they go? As a matter of fact, I believe that marriage is all benefit with minimal risks for women, whereas for men there is no guaranteed benefit and plenty of risks. That's why I guess women are whining over men's reluctance to tie the knots. Purabi, marriage is all good for women because it has so many beneficial strings attached to it.'

'I guess Raunaq is right, Purabi,' said Barkha. 'It was actually Anjali who made us realize that it is the homemaker who ultimately contributes to the growth of her family and eventually to society. There's no job like that of a housewife who works day in, day out for the sake of her family. There are no leaves or even a day off. It is the most exerting job in the world, yet there is no credit given to it. There's no one to understand the pain and struggle that she lives with. But still, work in silence is what a housewife does all throughout her life. And this, she does out of her own free will. There is no coercion involved.'

There was sheer silence in the hall until Purabi handed over the mike to Anjali. 'Will you please say something?' she requested. 'We all are waiting to hear you, dear.'

'I really feel blessed to have such friends,' said Anjali, clearing her throat. Her loud voice pierced through the silence. 'Actually, there is a lot that I want to say, but I am unable to find the words to express my feelings. I can only say thank you to these wonderful ladies for this honour and for everything else. As far as relationships are concerned, yes, I do agree with Raunaq. Let me tell you something. Being self-reliance can get exhausting. Making all the decisions is exhausting and so is the life of an alpha woman. Today, when more and more women are adapting an independent lifestyle, I have chosen this simple life for myself. You know why? Well, that's because it's liberating to become more beta. You tend to make happier relations once you understand your responsibilities towards them. Believe me, when both partners work full time, marriage has the potential to become a war zone. And this, I realized when I met Raunaq years back. If both partners are leading identical lives, it's only natural to try and keep score.'

'True,' said Raunaq in affirmation. 'Most marital conflicts amount to a simple power struggle. There are two people who wish to drive the same car. Well, that never works. The only way to put an end to this struggle is for one partner to take the passenger seat. Mind it, not the back seat. Just the passenger seat. Once you let go of your need to rule the world, believe me life becomes easier and the world becomes a better place to live in.'

'So if that is the case,' said Barkha chirpily, 'then why not, give the real achiever the credit for all her sacrifices? And with these words, I would like to reveal the exact reason for this celebration. Actually, Aradhya and I would like to dedicate the Women Achievers Award that we received two years back, to Anju for her exemplary contribution to her family and society. And ultimately, this award is for her ideologies that helped change our lives for the better. This award is for real woman power. And, this…' Barkha said holding the trophy in her hands, 'I dedicate to Anju!'

The hall was filled with applause as the ladies on stage hugged each other. Anju, who was unaware of the reason for this celebration till now, was unable to hold back her tears. She looked at Akhil and Raunaq, the men in her life who made her realize the importance of being a woman. 'Thank you both for everything! Had it not been for you, I would never have been the way I am today and I owe this achievement to you.'

While Akhil hugged her, Raunaq took the mike to express his exhilaration. 'Dear all, it's a big day for us! It's a moment to live! An evening to embrace and a night to be treasured forever. Well, the story behind tonight's event is a long one and I wouldn't take much of your time discussing it. All I would like to say is that giving this Woman Achievers Award to a homemaker is the best way to honour her. I am glad Barkha and Aradhya took this step today. Fr our generation is desperately trying to prove that women can do what men can do and it is so much engrossed in it, that women are losing their uniqueness today. As a matter of fact, women weren't created to do everything men can. They were created to do everything that men can't! Women are the main reason behind the happiness, or unhappiness, of families. And therefore, I am of the opinion that women of a household should be placed on a high pedestal. Even the government needs to consider "homemaking" as the noblest profession and instead of providing maternity leave and reservation to women, it should provide family pensions to homemakers. You see, it's an art of selfless giving, no less than the sacrifice made by army jawans and it needs to be compensated and respected by one and all.'

'I am also a working woman, sir, and you just said there's a long story behind this realization. Will you share that with us?' said a voice from the crowd.

'For that, you need to read *Just Don't Do It*! I think there's no better way to explain it,' replied Raunaq and winked at Anjali, who smiled back in affirmation.